Royal Borough of
Greenwich

**Abbey Wood Library
Eynsham Drive, SE2 9PT
020 8310 4185**

Thank you!

To renew, please contact any Royal
Greenwich library or renew online at
www.royalgreenwich.gov.uk/libraries

fantastical HATS & BEANIES

Jenny Occleshaw

NH
NEW
HOLLAND

Dedication

I would like to dedicate this book to my beautiful daughter Felicity who has survived all manner of peculiar knitted and crocheted creations throughout her life and has lived to tell the tale, and to Fin and Elsie who are an endless source of inspiration and joy in my life.

First published in 2012 by New Holland Publishers (UK) Ltd
London • Cape Town • Sydney • Auckland
www.newhollandpublishers.com

Garfield House	Wembley Square	Unit 1, 66 Gibbes Street	218 Lake Road
86-88 Edgware Road	First Floor, Solan	Chatswood	Northcote
London W2 2EA, UK	Road Gardens	New South Wales 2067	Auckland
	Cape Town 8001	Australia	New Zealand
	South Africa		

10 9 8 7 6 5 4 3 2 1

ISBN 978 1 74257 286 4
A catalogue record of this book is available at the National Library

Publishing Manager: Lliane Clarke
Senior Editor: Simona Hill
Photographer: Graham Gillies
Illustrator: Steve Dew
Designer: Kimberley Pearce
Production Director Olga Dementiev

Printed and bound Toppan Leefung (China) Ltd

Author's Note

Please enjoy making these patterns. They are not for commercial reproduction. For assistance with patterns contact Drop Stitch Designs (jennyoccleshaw@hotmail.com).

Publisher's Note

Some of the hats are made with small parts that may be a choking hazzard to a young child or baby. Ensure they are stitched firmly in place and check them regularly. If in doubt, do not add them to the hats.

Contents

Introduction

The hats and beanies in this book have all been made using either double knitting yarn (DK/8 ply) or 4-ply knitting yarn, the latter of which is generally used for baby knits, since it is fine thread. While I have generally not specified a particular brand I recommend that you use pure wool for these knits since it is resilient and also available in a broad range of lovely colours. Pure wool is warm and cosy to wear and is much kinder on knitter's hands. When using mohair yarns use the ply specified otherwise your hat may end up the wrong size.

These beanies are mostly knitted 'in the round', meaning that you will either work with three double-pointed needles, with the number of stitches split equally between the three needles, or you will use a circular needle. Circular needles are made to different lengths. Generally a loop of thick plastic holds the needles together. Make sure that you chooce a needle that is 40 cm long otherwise you will stretch the yarn too much in order to join the ends into a circle.

The average tension is approximately 22 stitches and 30 rows to 10 cm square when knitted using 4 mm knitting needles. If your tension is tight use slightly larger knitting needles and if your tension is loose use slightly smaller knitting needles.

When working with multiple yarns, make sure you carry the colours not in use behind the knitted work. Be careful not to pull the yarn too tightly or this will create a puckered effect. When joining in a new colour twist the two colours together at the back of the work so that you don't create a hole, and always leave a long tail of yarn at the start and end of any colour addition so that you have thread to darn in.

Stitch all decorative features on really securely. This cannot be overstated. Some of the hats have very small parts such as beads and buttons, which can be a hazzard for even the youngest baby. If in doubt, omit these details and embroider them instead with stranded embroidery cotton.

I recommend that you gather all your supplies together before you begin a project and take your time when knitting. Start with a simple project from the beginning of the book if you are a novice knitter and progress to more complex items as you gain confidence. Recipients of your hats will be absolutely thrilled so it's worth taking the time to get the designs just right.

Abbreviations

Beg; beginning
Cont: continue
Cm: centimetres
Dec: decrease
Inc: increase the number of stitches by knitting into the front and back of the next stitch
K: knit
M1 : make 1 stitch by picking up the loop that lies between the two needles and knitting into the back
P: purl
Psso: pass slip stitch over
Rep: repeat
Sl: slip
St: stitch or stitches
St st: stocking stitch
Rem: remaining
Rep: repeat
Rs: right side
Tbl: through back of loops
Tog: together
Work x tog: knit or purl x stitches together
Ws: wrong side
Yfwd: yarn forward
Yo: yarn over needle
Yrn: yarn round needle

Crochet Abbreviations

Ch: chain
Dc: double crochet
Ss: slip stitch
Tr: treble
Dtr: double treble
Htr: half treble

Busy Bee

This is a hat for a little baby, knitted in very soft baby wool. It's a simple ribbed knit with plenty of stretch for maximum comfort. Feelers and embroidered bees turn it into something very special. The embroidered bees are created using rows of embroidered bullion knots.

Size
To fit 6-9 months

Materials

1 x 50 g ball black 4-ply pure wool
1 x 50 g ball pale yellow 4-ply pure wool
Stranded embroidery cotton in white, black and yellow

3.25 mm knitting needles
Wool needle
Embroidery needle
Chenille pipe cleaners (optional)

Using 3.25 mm knitting needles, and black cast on 115 sts.
Work in k1, p1 rib and stripe pattern as follows until work measures 14 cms from cast-on edge:
4 rows rib: black
4 rows rib: pale yellow

Crown Shaping
Maintain stripe pattern and at the same time:
Dec row: Rib 2, (work 3 tog, rib 3), 18 times, work 3 tog, rib 2.
Rib 3 rows without shaping.
Dec row: Rib 1, (work 3 tog, rib 1), 19 times.
Dec row: Rib 1, (rib 2 tog) to end (20 sts).
Break off yarn. Thread through rem sts, pull up tightly and fasten off.
Join seam, reversing seam at lower third to allow for turning brim.

Feelers
Using 3.25 mm knitting needles and black, cast on 7 sts.
Beg with a knit row, work in st st for 7 cm. Cast off.

To Make Up Roll up lengthwise. Insert a chenille pipe cleaner into each feeler and stitch closed. This is not strictly necessary, but does make the bee's feelers stand straight. Attach the feelers to the top of the hat spacing them evenly. Ensure that the stitching is firm.

Embroidering Bees
There are 9 knitted bees on the baby hat, 4 on the brim and 5 on the body of the hat. Use pins to mark the positions for your bees so that you are happy with the placement.

Using 3 strands of black embroidery cotton, make a 6-wrap bullion knot for the tail. Leave a little space.
Make a 9-wrap bullion knot parallel to the first, leaving the width of one bullion knot between the stitches. Leave a little space.
Make a 7-wrap bullion knot. Leave a little space.
Make a 5-wrap bullion knot for the head.
Work 2 straight stitches as feelers protruding at angles from the top of the head.
Using 3 strands of yellow embroidery cotton and starting at the tail end of the bee, make an 8-wrap bullion knot in the space between the 6- and the 9-wrap bullion knots.
Make an 11-wrap bullion knot in

the space between the 9- and the
7-wrap bullion knots.
Make an 8-wrap bullion knot in the
space between the 7 and 5-wrap
bullion knots.

Wings

Using 3 strands of white
embroidery cotton, bring the
needle out at the 11-wrap yellow
bullion stitch. Make 2 lazy daisy
stitches on each side of the bee's
body for wings.

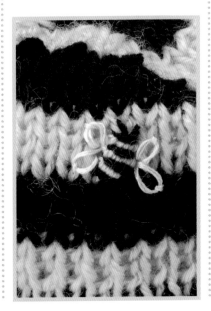

Apple Blossom

This is a delightful hat for any little girl who loves pink. The ruffles are crocheted onto the hat base once the hat is knitted. Little beaded flowers are stitched onto the crown, though they can be left off if you think they are likely to be chewed or pulled off.

Sizes

To fit 18 months to 2 years (3 to 4 years)

Materials

1 x 50 g ball bright pink DK (8-ply) wool
1 x 50 g ball pale pink DK (8-ply) wool
1 x 50 g ball cream DK (8-ply) wool
Small amounts of bright pink and cream 4-ply wool for the flowers

6 (7) crystal beads for the flower centres
4 mm double-pointed knitting needles
Wool needle
3 mm crochet hook
White sewing cotton
Beading needle

Using the 4 mm double-pointed circular knitting needles and bright pink, cast on 90 (100) sts. Join into a ring, being careful not to twist the stitches. Thread a loop of a different colour wool onto the needle to indicate the start/end of a row. Work 10 rounds in st st.

Break off the bright pink and join in the pale pink. Knit 1 round.

Join in the cream wool.

Work 12 rounds of k1, p1 rib, alternating the colours with each stitch and beginning with k1 in pale pink. Twist the threads neatly at the back of the work.

Break off pale pink and continue in cream.

Next round: Purl.

Work 10 rounds st st (every round knit).

Next round: Purl.
Work 8 rounds st st.
Next round: Purl.
Work 6 rounds st st.
Next round: Purl.
Work 3 rounds st st.
Next round: Purl.

Crown Shaping

Join in pale pink. The crown is worked in alternating rounds of cream and pale pink.

Next round : *K7 (8), k2tog, rep from * to end of round.
Next round: Knit.
Next round : *K6 (7), k2tog, rep from * to end of round.
Next round: Knit.
Next round : *K5 (6), k2tog, rep from * to end of round.
Next round : *K4(5), k2tog, rep from * to end of round.
Next round: Knit.
Next round : *K3(4), k2tog, rep from * to end of round.
Next round: Knit.
Next round : *K2(3), k2tog, rep from * to end of round.
Next round: Knit.
Continue decreasing in this manner until the round k2tog all round has been worked.

Break off yarn, thread through rem sts, pull up tightly and fasten off. Sew in all the ends on the wrong side.

Ruffles

The ruffles are crocheted in rounds of pale pink and bright pink. They are worked into the purl rows knitted into the body of the hat. Work from the brim up.

With a 3 mm crochet hook and pale pink, insert the hook into the first purl loop of the purl row at the top of the rib.

* Work 3 ch, dc into next purl loop, rep from * all the way around the hat finishing with a sl st into first st. Continue in this manner until all 5 rounds of crochet have been worked.

Flowers

(Make 6 for the smaller size, and 7 for the larger size in a combination of deep pink for the outer flowers and cream for the inner flowers.

Using a 3 mm crochet hook make 4ch, join into a ring with a ss.

1st round: (right side) 2ch, 9dc in ring, ss to top of 2ch (10 sts).

2nd round: 5ch, 1tr in each of next 9dc, ss to top of 5ch. Fasten off. Darn in ends and form into a neat circle.

Using a beading needle threaded with white cotton, very firmly stitch 1 crystal bead to the centre of each flower.

To Make Up

Stitch one flower to the centre of the crown and distribute the other flowers evenly around the crown. Stitch firmly in place.

Little Ladybird

This is a simple hat is ideal for less experienced knitters and is perfect for babies to wear. The ladybird's spots are bobbles, which are made separately and attached once the beanie is complete.

Size
To fit 6-9 months

Materials
1 x 50 g ball red 4-ply wool
Small amount of black 4-ply wool
3.25 mm knitting needles
2 mm knitting needles
Wool needle

Using 3.25 mm knitting needles, and red, cast on 115 sts.
Work in k1, p1 rib until work measures 14 cms from beg.

Shape Top

Dec row: Rib 2, (work 3 tog, rib 3), 18 times, work 3 tog, rib 2.
Rib 3 rows without shaping.
Dec row: Rib 1, (work 3 tog, rib 1), 19 times.
Dec row: Rib 1, (rib2tog) to end (20 sts).
Break off yarn. Thread through rem sts, pull up tightly and fasten off.
Join seam, reversing seam at lower third to allow for turning up of brim.

Bobbles

Using 2 mm knitting needles and black cast on 1 st.
K1, p1, k1, p1, k1 all in to same st (5 sts).
Next row: Purl
Next row: Knit.
Next row: Purl
Next row: Knit, *pass second st over first on right-hand needle, rep from * until 1 st rem. Fasten off.
Make 12.

To Make Up Run a gathering thread around the edge of the bobble and draw up to form a round bobble. Sew in one end and use the other to attach the bobble to the beanie.
Attach one to the top of the crown and stitch the others randomly around the hat. Turn up the brim.

Baby Flowers

This is a simple hat for a young baby. It's knitted from very soft 4-ply baby yarn and is a good choice for a novice to knit. The gorgeous felt flowers brighten the design, use just one colour or have a whole array of beautiful blooms. Felted flowers are available from craft shops and haberdashers or online from speciality felt suppliers.

Size
To fit 6-9 months

Materials
1 x 50 g ball cream 4-ply pure
    baby wool
3.25 mm knitting needles
Wool needle
10 felt flowers, 4 cm in diameter
Sewing cotton and needle

Using 3.25 mm knitting needles and cream cast on 115 sts.
Work in k1, p1 rib until work measures 14 cm from cast on row.

Shape Top

Dec row: Rib 2, (rib 3 tog, rib 3), 18 times, work 3 tog, rib 2 (79 sts).

Rows 1-4: Work 3 rows of rib without shaping.

Row 5: Rib 1, (rib 3 tog, rib 1), 19 times (41 sts).

Row 6: Rib 1, (Rib 2 tog) to end (20 sts).

Break off yarn. Thread through rem sts, pull up tightly and fasten off.

To Make Up

Join the seam, alternating the stitching of the seam on the lower third to allow for turning up the brim.

Turn up the brim for 3.5 cm. Arrange the felt flowers around the hat as desired and pin in place. Stitch into position and tie off. Each needs to be sewn on individually, otherwise the hat will lose its stretch. Try not to go through too many knitted stitches when sewing on the flowers

Cheeky Elf

Most of my inspiration for knitting projects come from my small grandchildren. There is nothing more satisfying than knitting for those you love. Their adorable elfin faces will look just lovely framed by this elfin hat. Noro variegated yarn provides the colour striping and little knitted leaves add extra detail. The hat is knitted in the round and finished with a cheeky knot.

Sizes

To fit 12 months (2-3 years)

Materials

1 x 100 g ball Noro sock yarn colour S220.
3.25 mm double-pointed knitting needles
2 x 2.25mm double-pointed knitting needles
Wool needle

Using 3.25 mm double-pointed needles, and Noro sock yarn, cast on 92 (112) sts (30, 32, 30 / 37, 38, 37) sts. Join into a ring being careful not to twist the stitches. Work 10 rounds st st for rolled brim.

Next round: Work 10 rounds k1, p1 rib.

Continue to work in st st (every row knit) until work measures 13 (14) cm.

Crown Shaping

Next round: *K21 (26), k2tog, rep from * to end of row.

Alt rounds: Knit.

Next round: *K20 (25), k2tog, rep from * to end of row.

Cont decreasing in this manner until 12 sts rem. Work on these 12 sts for 5 cm.

Next round: K1, k2tog, k1, k2tog, k1, k2tog, k1, k2tog (8 sts).

Cont on these 8 sts until top knot measures 15 cm in total.

Next round: K2tog all round. Break off yarn. Thread through rem sts, pull up tightly and fasten off.

To Make Up

Sew in any loose ends and press lightly if needed. Knot the top knot.

I-Cord Leaves

(Make 8 from Noro Sock yarn.) Using 2 x 2.25 mm double-pointed knitting needles, cast on 3 sts. Make an I-Cord as follows:

Row 1: *Knit, pull sts to the other end of needle, pull yarn firmly behind. Rep from * until I-Cord is 3 cm. Now work backwards and forwards in rows

Row 2: K1, yfwd, k1, yfwd, k1.

Row 3 and odd rows: Knit.

Row 4: K2, yfwd, k1, yfwd, k2.

Row 6: K3, yfwd, k1, yfwd, k3.

Row 8: K4, yfwd, k1, yfwd, k4.

Row 10: K5, yfwd, k1, yfwd, k5.

Row 12: Sl1, k1, psso, k9, k2tog.

Row 14: Sl1, k1, psso, k7, k2tog.

Row 16: Sl1, k1, psso, k5, k2tog.

Row 18: Sl1, k1, psso, k3, k2tog.

Row 20: Sl1, k1, psso, k1, k2tog.

Row 22: Sl2, k1, psso, fasten off.

To Make Up Press lightly if needed. Sew in ends.

Stitch the leaves at random around the hat.

The Great Gatsby

This beret, scarf and shoes set reminds me of the tweed caps worn in the 1920s. I wanted to make some patterns that were specifically for boys and I think this is most definitely one of them. The little Fair Isle band and the loops on the crown give the design a more contemporary feel. This is a fairly simple knit.

Size
To fit 6-9 months

Materials
3 x 50 g balls tweedy brown DK (8 ply)
Small amounts of DK (8 ply) in cream, olive green and fawn
3.75 mm knitting needles
3 mm knitting needles
Stitch holder
3 mm double-pointed knitting needles
Wool needle

Beret

Using 3.75 mm and tweedy brown, cast on 75 sts.

Work in k1, p1 rib for 7 rows.

Inc row: K4, (m1, k1, m1, k10) 6 times, m1, k1, m1, k3, m1, k1 (90 sts).

Work the Fair Isle Pattern rows 1–7 as follows:

Fair Isle Pattern

(10 st repeat, worked over 7 rows)

C: Cream
F: Fawn
G: Olive green

Row 1: K1C, k1G, k4C, k1F k3C

Row 2: P2C, p3F, p2C, p3G.

Row 3: K1G, k1C, k2G, k2C, k1F, k2C, k1G.

Row 4: P2G, p3C, p2G, p3C.

Row 5: K1C, k1F, k2C, k2G, k1C, k2G, k1C.

Row 6: P2C, p3G, p2C, p3F.

Row 7: K1C, k1F, k4C, k1G, k4C.

Continuing in tweedy brown and st st purl one row, decreasing 1 st (89 sts).

Inc row: K5, (m1, k1, m1, k12) 6 times, m1, k1, m1, k5. Work 5 rows st st (103 sts).

Inc row: K6, (m1, k1, m1, k14) 6 times, m1, k1, m1, k6 (117 sts). Work 5 rows st st.

Continue increasing 14 sts on the next and every following sixth row until there are 159 sts.

Work another 5 rows st st.

Dec row: K8, (k2tog, k1, k2tog, k18) 6 times, k2tog, k1, k2tog, k8. Work 5 rows st st.

Dec row: K7, (k2tog, k1, k2tog, k16) 6 times, k2tog, k1, k2tog, k7. Work 5 rows st st.

Dec row: K6, (k2tog, k1, k2tog, k14) 6 times, k2tog, k1, k2tog, k6. Work 5 rows st st.

Cont decreasing 14 sts on each dec row until 33 sts rem.

Next row: Purl.

Next row: K1, (k2tog) to end.

Next row: Purl.

Next row: K1, (k2tog) to end. Break off yarn, thread through rem sts, pull up tightly and fasten off.

To Make Up

Press lightly, if needed. Sew in all ends and using back stitch or mattress stitch sew seam.

I-Cord Loops

(Make 3 x 10cm long, 1 using cream, 1 using olive green and 1 using fawn.

Using 3 mm double-pointed knitting needles and DK (8-ply) yarn cast on 3 sts and knit an I-Cord to required length. Sl1, k2tog, psso. Break off yarn and draw through rem st.

Fasten off neatly. Loops can be made in different sizes, if you like. Attach loops firmly to top of crown.

Shoes

Sole

Using 3 mm knitting needles and tweedy brown, cast on 3 sts. Work in garter st for the sole of the shoe. Inc 1 st at each end of rows 2, 3, 5, 6 and 8 (13 sts).

Work another 28 rows without shaping.

Dec 1 st at each end of next and following alt rows until 5 sts rem.

Upper

Continuing in stocking stitch.

Row 1: Inc in first 2 sts, k1, inc in rem 2 sts (9 sts).

Even rows: Purl.

Row 3: *K1, inc in next 2 sts, k1 * twice, k1 (13 sts).

Row 5: *K2, inc in next 2 sts, k2, * twice, k1 (17 sts).

Row 7: K3, inc, k8, inc, k4 (19 sts).

Row 9: Knit.

Row 10: (*P2, inc*) twice, p6, inc, p2,* inc, twice, p1 (23 sts).

Work another 15 rows without shaping.

Row 26: K10, cast off 3sts, k10.

Row 28: K1, k2tog, k7.

Row 30: K1, k2tog, k6.

Row 32: K1, k2tog, k5.

Work another 14 rows without shaping. Cast off.

Rejoin yarn to the other side at centre front.

Next row: K7, sl1, k1, psso.

Cont decreases as set and work to match the other side.

Edging

With right side facing, using 3 mm knitting needles and olive green, pick up and knit 35 sts around foot opening. Cast off.

To Make Up

Join heel seam. Pin the foot to the top and ease in any excess. Stitch into position. Turn right side out. Make 2 x 8 cm I-Cord loops for each shoe, 1 cream and 1 fawn.

Scarf

Using 3.75 mm knitting needles and tweedy brown, cast on 24 sts. Work 7 rows k1, p1 rib. Coninue in garter stitch. Work 4 rows cream. 4 rows fawn and 4 rows olive green. Work 190 rows tweedy brown.

Next row: Knit 12, turn, continue on these 12 sts and work 20 rows. Rejoin yarn to remain 12st and work 20 rows on these sts. Now work across all 24 sts. You will have a large 'buttonhole' in the middle of the scarf. Work another 50 rows garter st.

Next row: Work 4 rows olive green, 4 rows fawn, 4 rows cream.

Next row: Work 7 rows k1, p1 rib. Cast off in rib.

Tuck one end of scarf through the buttonhole.

Ladybird, Ladybird

Who doesn't love ladybirds? This beanie is a simple design in striking red and black. The ladybirds are knitted separately and stitched on once the hat is complete. Made up in the same wool as the hat, there is no requirement to have oddments of yarn, making this a good project for a beginner.

Sizes

To fit 18 months to 2 years (3-4 years)

Materials

1 x 50 g ball black DK (8 ply)
1 x 50 g ball red wool DK (8 ply)
Polyester fibre filling
4 mm double-pointed knitting needles

3 mm knitting needles
Wool needle
Black stranded embroidery cotton
Embroidery needle

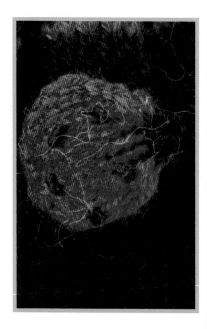

Using 4 mm double-pointed knitting needle and black, cast on 92 (102) sts. Join into a ring being careful not to twist the stitches. Work 10 rounds st st (knit every round).

Break off black and join in red. Work in k2, p2 rib for 12 rounds. Break off red and join in black.

Next round: Working in st st dec 2 sts evenly on this round (90 / 100 sts).

Cont in st st until work measures 16 (17) cm from beg of rolled brim.

Crown Shaping

Work alternating rounds of red and black.

Round 1: *K7 (8), k2tog, rep from * to end of round.

Round 2: Knit.

Round 3: *K6 (7), k2tog, rep from

* to end of round.

Round 4: Knit.

Round 5: *K5 (6), k2tog, rep from * to end of round.

Continue decreasing in this manner until the round k2tog all round has been worked.

Break off yarn, thread through rem sts, pull up tightly and fasten off. Sew in all ends carefully on wrong side.

Ladybird

Using 3 mm knitting needles and red cast on 3 sts for the lower body.

Row 1: Inc once in each of first two sts, k1 (5 sts).

Row 2 and all even rows: Purl.**

Row 3: Inc in first, (k1, m1) twice, inc in next st, k1 (9 sts).

Row 5: Inc in first st, k3, m1, k1, m1,

k2, inc in next st, k1 (13 sts).

Row 7: Knit.

Row 9: (K1, sl1, k1, psso) twice, k1, (k2tog, k1) twice (9 sts).

Row 11: K1, sl2, psso, k1, k2tog, slip stitch just made back on to left-hand needle, pass next st over it slip st back on to right-hand needle, k1 (5 sts).

Change to black for the head.

Row 13: Sl2, k1, psso, k1 (3 sts).

Row 14: Sl1, p2tog, psso, fasten off.

Underside

Using 3 mm knitting needles and black cast on 3 sts for the lower body.

Row 1: Inc once in each of first two sts, k1 (5 sts).

Row 2 and all even rows: Purl.**

Row 3: Inc in first st, k2, inc in next st, k1 (7 sts).

Rows 5 and 7: Knit.
Row 9: K1, sl1, k1, psso, k1, k2tog, k1 (5 sts).
Row 11: Sl2, k1, psso, k1 (3 sts).
Row 12: Sl1, p2tog, psso, fasten off. Make 7.

To Make Up

Using 6 strands of black embroidery cotton, embroider 5 spots on the upper side of the ladybird using bullion knots.
With wrong sides together join upper body to underside, using very small stitches. When half way round insert a small amount of polyester fibre filling. Don't make the ladybirds too fat.
Attach one ladybird firmly to the top of the crown and place the other six at intervals around the hat.

Moonbeam

A colourful take on the traditional nightcap shape. This warm woolly hat will keep little heads cosy with its wide ribbed band, tapering shape and, for a bit of extra fun, some knitted balls attached to I-Cords. This is a simple design knitted on two needles. You could also make it in a solid colour or go crazy and add more stripes.

Sizes

To fit 1-2 years (3-4 years)

Materials

1 x 50 g ball red DK (8 ply)
1 x 50 g ball white DK (8 ply)
Small amount of red and white
  4 ply

Polyester fibre filling
2.75 mm knitting needles
3.25 mm knitting needles
4 mm knitting needles

Tension

22 sts and 28 rows to 10 cm square measured over st st on 4mm knitting needles.

Abbreviation

Wrap: Bring yarn to front, slip next st from left to right needle, take yarn to back of work, return st to left-hand needle. This prevents holes in the work when turning.

Using 3.25 mm knitting needles and red 8 ply, cast on 96 (108) sts. Work 20 rows in k1, p1 rib. Change to 4 mm knitting needles. Join in white 8 ply. Commence striped pattern, 2 rows red, 2 rows white and work in st st until work measures 12 (14) cm from beg, ending with a purl row.

Shape Top

Dec Row: K22 (25), k2tog tbl, k2tog, k22 (25) twice.
Work 3 rows st st without shaping.
Dec Row: K21 (24), k2tog tbl, k2tog, k21 (24) twice.
Work 3 rows st st without shaping.
Dec Row: K20 (23), k2tog tbl, k2tog, k20 (23) twice.
Work 3 rows st st without shaping. Cont decreasing in this manner on every 4th row as set until 20 sts rem. Work another 3 rows without shaping.
Next row: K2tog all across row. Break off yarn, thread through rem sts pull up tightly and fasten off.

Knitted Balls

Using 2.75mm double-pointed knitting needles and 4 ply, cast on 12 sts.
Row 1: Knit.
Row 2: P10, wrap.
Row 3: K8, wrap.
Row 4: P6, wrap.
Row 5: K4, wrap.
Row 6: Purl.
Rep these 6 rows another 4 times. Cast off.

With right sides together sew side seam half way. Turn right side out and stuff firmly with polyester fibre filling. Sew the rest of the seam and then run a gathering thread around the cast-on edge. Pull up firmly and fasten off. Do the same with the other end.
Make 2 red balls and 2 white balls.

I-Cords

Using 2.75mm double-pointed knitting needles and red DK (8 ply), cast on 3 sts and then commence the I-Cord. Knit the stitches, slide them to the end of the needle, pull the yarn firmly behind and knit the stitches again, continuing in this manner until each cord is the desired length. K2tog, psso. Fasten off. Make 2 white I-Cords, 11 and 13 cm long, and 2 red I-Cords, 12 and 14 cm long.

To Make Up

Press lightly if needed. Sew centre back seam using back stitch or mattress stitch. Sew in any ends. Sew a white I-Cord to a red ball and a red ball to a white I-Cord. Repeat for the other 2 balls. Firmly sew to the point of the hat.

Baby Jester

This little jester's cap looks complicated but really isn't too difficult to make. Knitted in the round, it divides at the crown and continues in two halves to shape the peaks. The colours are reversed in the peaks for added interest. Knitted balls and I-Cords make this a splendid little hat.

Size
To fit 6–9 months

Materials
1 x 50 g ball blue 4 ply
1 x 50 g ball cream 4 ply
Small amount extra blue 4 ply
    for knitted balls and I-Cords
3.25 mm double-pointed
    circular knitting needles
2 mm knitting needles

1 stitch holder
2 sets 2 mm double-pointed
    knitting needles
Wool needle
Small amount of polyester
    fibre filling

Using 3.25 mm double-pointed circular knitting needles and blue, cast on 124 sts. Join into a ring, being careful not to twist the stitches. Mark the end of the row with a loop of different colour wool.

Work in k2, p2 rib for 32 rounds. The striped pattern is made up of 6 rows worked as follows:

Knit 4 rounds blue.

Knit 1 round cream.

Purl 1 round blue.

Continue working striped pattern until work measures 18 cm.

Crown Shaping

Place the first 62 st of the round on a stitch holder. Working with the rem 62 stitches continue in rounds joining the end of the row to the start of the next and marking the start/finish of the round with a different colour loop of wool. Work 3 rounds blue, decreasing 2 sts evenly on the first round. Work 1 round cream and another 4 rounds blue.

Dec round: Using cream k2tog, k26, k2tog tbl, k2tog, k26, k2tog tbl.

Next round: Purl using cream.

Next round: Knit using cream. Work 4 rounds blue st st.

Dec round: Using cream k2tog, k24, k2tog tbl, k2tog, k24, k2tog tbl.

Next round: Purl using cream.

Next round: Knit using cream. Work 4 rounds blue st st.

Dec round: Using cream k2tog, k22, k2tog tbl, k2tog, k22, k2tog tbl.

Continue decreasing 2 stitches on each decrease round until 40 stitches remain, then decrease on every other stripe until 12 stitches remain.

Next round: K2tog all around. Break off yarn, thread through remaining sts, pull up tightly and fasten off.

Place the stitches on the needle holder back on double-pointed circular needles and rejoin yarn to centre front of hat. Commence knitting at this point.

Complete to match first side reversing colours.

Knitted Balls

Using 2 mm needles cast on 12 sts using cream.

Row 1: Knit

Row 2: P10, wrap.

Row 3: K8, wrap.

Row 4: P6, wrap.

Row 5: K4, wrap.

Row 6: Purl.

Rep these 6 rows 4 times. Cast off. With right sides together sew side seam half way. Turn the right way out and stuff firmly. Sew the remainder of the seam and then run a gathering thread around the cast on edge. Pull up firmly and fasten off. Do the same with the other end. Make 1 more with blue.

To Make Up

Sew in all ends. Stitch up the opening on the crown between the start of the knitted two points. Sew a blue ball to a cream I-Cord and stitch this and two knotted I-Cords to the end of one point. Repeat using the remaining I-Cords and knitted ball on the other hat point. Press lightly with a warm iron, but be careful not to flatten the ribbed pattern. Turn up the brim and knot the two peaks in a loose knot.

I-Cords

Make 6 I-cords, 2 x 12 cm long to attach to the knitted balls and 4 x 10 cm long to knot. Make half blue and half cream.
Using 2 mm double-pointed knitting needles and blue, cast on 3 sts. Knit 1 row, slide the stitches to the opposite end of the needle, pull the yarn firmly behind and knit the stitches again, continuing in this manner until each cord is the desired length. K2tog, psso, fasten off.

Slippers

Using 3 mm knitting needles and French blue 4 ply, cast on 3 sts. Work in garter st.

Inc 1 st at each end of rows 2, 3, 5, 6 and 8 (13 sts).

Work another 28 rows in garter stitch without shaping.

Next row: Dec 1 st at each end of next and 3 foll alt rows until 5 sts rem.

Top of Slipper

Row 1: Inc in first 4 sts, k1 (9 sts).
Row 2 and all even rows: Purl.
Row 3: K1, inc in each of next 2 sts, k2, inc in each of next 2 sts, k2 (13 sts).
Row 5: K2, inc in next 2 sts, k4, inc in next 2 sts, k3 (17 sts).
Row 7: K3, inc in next st, k8, inc in next st, k4 (19 sts).

Row 8: Purl.
Row 9: Knit.
Row 10: (P2, inc) twice, p6, (inc, p2) twice, p1 (23 sts).
Work 14 rows without shaping
Row 25: K10, cast off 3sts, k10.
Row 27: K1, k2tog, knit to end.
Row 29: As row 27.
Row 31: As row 27.
Work another 15 rows st st without shaping.
Cast off.
Rejoin yarn to rem sts at centre front.
Row 26: (wrong side) purl.
Row 27: Knit to last 3 sts, k2tog, k1.
Complete as for first side.

Sock

Using 3 mm knitting needles and white 4 ply, pick up and knit 41 sts around foot opening.
Work 20 rows k1, p1 rib. Break off white and join in blue 4 ply. Work 3 rows in k1, p1, rib. Cast off in rib.

To Make Up Using mattress stitch, join heel and sock seam. With right sides together pin top of slipper to sole. Stitch all the way around. Turn right side out.

Bows

Using 3 mm knitting needles and blue 4 ply, cast on 14 sts. Work 20 rows st st, commencing with a knit row. Cast off. Make up as for the hat. Attach one bow firmly to the top of each slipper.

Pearly Queen

Usually I wouldn't put buttons on a hat for a little one in case they accidentally found their way into their mouths. However, because this is for a baby, who is unlikely to remove buttons of their own accord I indulged a flight of fancy in this confection. Made with very soft 4-ply baby wool it is simple to make and will keep your little one's head snuggly warm.

Size
To fit 3–9 months

Materials
1 x 50 g ball cream 4 ply
20 tiny pale pink buttons
100 tiny cream buttons
75 cm pink ribbon
3.25mm knitting needles

lower third to allow for turning up of brim.

Buttons
Sew pink buttons on the crown and cream ones lower down. Each button is sewn on individually or the hat will lose its stretch. Make sure all buttons are sewn on very firmly. Turn up brim and thread ribbon through eyelets.

Using 3.25 mm knitting needles, and cream cast on 115 sts.
Work in k1, p1 rib until work measures 2 cm.
Eyelet row: Rib 1, *yrn, rib2tog, rep from * to end.
Work in k1, p1 rib until work measures 14 cms from beg.

Shape Top
Dec row: Rib 2, (work 3 tog, rib 3), 18 times, work 3 tog, rib 2.
Rib 3 rows without shaping.
Dec row: Rib 1, (work 3 tog, rib 1), 19 times.
Dec row: Rib 1, (rib2tog) to end (20 sts).
Break off yarn. Thread through rem sts, pull up tightly and fasten off.
Join seam, reversing stitching at

Black Magic

Fun and sophisticated at the same time, this soft black hat is perfect for a special occasion. Made with black mohair and velvet it has a luxury quality, but the polka dot knitted balls stop it from looking too grown up.

Size
To fit 18 months to 2 years

Materials
1 x 50 g ball black DK (8 ply)
Small amount white DK (8 ply)
Small amount black mohair DK (8 ply)
75 cm of 1 cm-wide white velvet ribbon
Black and white stranded embroidery cottons
Polyester fibre filling
3.75 mm double-pointed knitting needles
1 pair of 3 mm knitting needles
Wool needle
Embroidery needle

Abbreviations

Wrap: Bring yarn to front, slip next st from left to right needle, take yarn to back of work, return st to left-hand needle. This prevents holes in the work when turning.
Mb (Make bobble): K1, p1, k1, p1, k1 into same st, turn, purl, turn knit, turn purl, turn, sl1, k1 *psso, k1, rep from * until 1 st rems.

Using 3.75mm double-pointed knitting needles and DK (8-ply) black mohair, cast on 92 sts on 3 needles (30, 32, 30).
Work 10 rounds st st.
Break off mohair and join in black DK (8 ply).
Work 13 rounds k2, p2 rib.
Rounds 4 and 5: Knit, dec 2 sts on 2nd needle of first round (90 sts).
Eyelet round: K1, *yrn twice, k2tog,

rep from * to end of round.
Round 7: Knit dropping the second wrap of yrn twice off the needle as you knit.
Continue in st st until work measures 12 cm from rolled-up brim.
Next round: Purl.
Work 2 rounds st st.
Bobble round: *K4, mb, rep from * to end of round.
Work another 2 rounds st st.
Next round: Purl.
Work 3 rounds st st. Break off black and join in white.

Crown Shaping
Round 1: *K7, k2tog, rep from * to end.
Round 2 and all even rounds: Knit in striped pattern.

Round 3: *K6, k2tog, rep from * to end.
Round 5: *K5, k2tog, rep from * to end.
Keeping pattern of decreasing continue in this manner until the round k1, k2tog has been worked. Break off yarn. Thread through rem sts, pull up tight and fasten off.

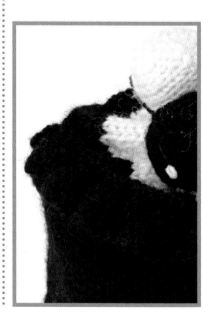

To Make Up

Thread velvet ribbon through the eyelet holes and tie into a bow. Attach the balls to the top of the hat, securing firmly. Sew in all ends.

Knitted Balls

Using 3 mm needles and black, cast on 12 sts.

Row 1: Knit.

Row 2: P10, wrap.

Row 3: K8, wrap.

Row 4: P6, wrap.

Row 5: K4, wrap.

Row 6: Purl.

Rep these 6 rows 4 times. Cast off. Using 3 strands of embroidery cotton make a bullion knot with 18–20 wraps. Form into a circle. Secure with a couple of tiny stitches so it maintains a circular shape. Work several more bullion knots at random over the knitted piece.

With right sides together sew the side seam half way. Turn the right way out and stuff firmly. Sew the remainder of the seam and then run a gathering thread around the cast on edge. Pull up firmly and fasten off. Do the same with the other end. Making sure you have sufficient filling and have made a round firm ball. Make 5 balls in total, 3 in black and 2 in white.

Coconut Ice

A lovely pastel beanie in the shades of coconut ice, with a rolled mohair brim and adorned with kid mohair flowers to give it a very luxurious feel. It is perfect for the little princess who loves all things pink and flowery. If using the seed pearl beads in the centre of the flowers be sure to stitch them down very firmly so they can't be pulled or bitten off.

Size

To fit 18 months to 2 1/2 years

Materials

1 x 50 g ball cream DK (8 ply)
1 x 50 g ball palest pink DK (8 ply)
Small amount DK (8 ply) pale pink mohair
25 g ball Rowan Kid Silk Haze pink

Pearl glass seed beads
3.75 mm double-pointed knitting needles
3 x 2.25 mm double-pointed knitting needles
Wool needle

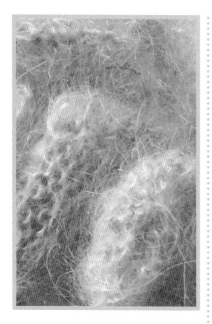

Abbreviation

Mb (make bobble) as follows: k1, p1, k1, p1, k1 into same st, turn, purl, turn and knit, turn and purl, turn, sl1, k1 *psso, k1, rep from * until 1 st rems.

Hat

Using 3.75 mm double-pointed knitting needles and pink mohair, cast on 90 sts evenly on three needles (30, 30, 30).
Work 10 rounds st st.
Break off mohair and join in cream.
Work in k1, p1 rib for 12 rounds.
Work 2 rounds st st in cream.
Join in pale pink 8 ply.

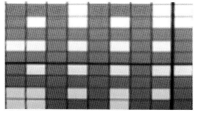

Work from the graph above, repeating it 10 times in total across the 90 stitches. Carry threads along the back of the work.
Work another 3 rounds st st in cream.
Knit 2 rounds pale pink.
Work 2 rounds st st using cream.
Bobble round: Using cream *k4, mb, rep from * to end of round.
Work another 2 rounds st st.
Next round: Knit 1 round pale pink
Next round: Purl 1 round pale pink.
Work 2 rounds st st using cream.
Knit 2 rounds pale pink.

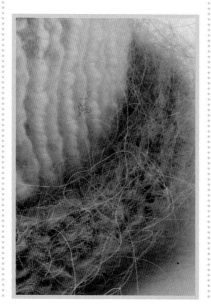

Work 2 rounds st st using cream.

Crown Shaping
Rest of hat is worked in cream.
Round 1: *K7, k2tog, rep from * to end.
Round 2 and even rounds: Knit.
Round 3: *K6, k2tog, rep from * to end.
Round 5: *K5, k2tog, rep from * to end.
Continue decreasing in this manner until the round k1, k2tog has been worked. Break off yarn. Thread through rem sts, pull up tight and fasten off.

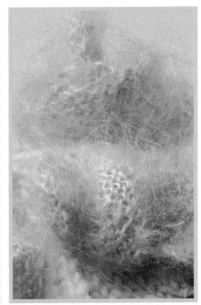

Flowers

Wind off a separate small ball of pale pink Kid Silk Haze as these flowers are worked from 2 strands of wool. To make a petal, using 2.25 mm double-pointed knitting needles, cast on 3 sts. Using the newly wound ball of wool and same needles cast on 3 sts (6 sts).

Row 1: (right side) K1, inc twice in next st, k1. Rep with next set of sts (5 sts) each set.

Row 2: Purl each set.

Row 3: K1, m1, k3, m1, k1. (7 sts in each set.

Row 4: Join the 2 sets together by purling them together side by side as follows: p6, p2tog, p6.

Row 5: K1, m1, k11, m1, k1 (15 sts).

Rows 6 , 8 , 10, 12 and 14: Purl.

Row 7: K6, sl2, k1, psso, k6 (13 sts).

Row 9: K5, sl2, k1, psso, k5 (11 sts).

Row 11: Sl2, k1, psso, k2, sl2, k1, psso, k2, k2tog (7 sts).

Row 13: Sl1, k1, psso, sl2, k1, psso, k2tog (3 sts).

Leave these 3 sts on a spare needle. Make three more petals for each flower setting aside each petal on the spare needle. Run a thread tightly through the 12 sts connecting the 4 petals and tie off. Stitch the pearl bead securely in the centre of the flower.

Make 5 flowers.

To Make Up

Sew in all ends. Attach flowers to crown and sides of hat, as desired.

Feathered Fancy

This beanie is inspired by a 1920's cloche hat, with its domed shape and feathers and flower decoration. A ribbon trim gives an extra touch of whimsy. Simple stitches combine to make this hat easy to knit but spectacular to look at and wear.

Size
To fit 2-3 years

Materials
1 x 50 g ball purple
Small amounts of DK (8-ply) pure wool in dusky pink, pale pink, dark pink (DP), pale purple (PP), bright pink and cream
1 m x 1 cm-wide bright pink ribbon

3 feathers
4 mm double-pointed knitting needles
Wool needle
3 mm crochet hook

Using 4 mm double-pointed knitting needles and pale purple, cast on 92 sts (30, 32, 30). Join into a ring, being careful not to twist the sts.

Work 10 rounds st st.

Join in dusky pink and work 14 rounds k2, p2 rib. Break off dusky pink.

Next round: Knit, dec 2 sts evenly on second needle.

Next round: Purl.

Next round: Knit.

Next round: Purl.

Eyelet round: *Knit, wrapping yarn twice around needle before knitting the stitch.

Next round: Knit, dropping the 2 wrapped stitches off the needle.

Next round: Purl.

Next round: Knit.

Break off pale purple and join in dark pink (DP) and pale pink (PP).

Next round: K3 DP, *k3 PP, rep from * to end of round.

Rep this round once.

Next round: K3 PP, *k3 DP, rep from * to end of round.

Rep this round once.

Next round: K3 DP, *k3 PP, rep from * to end of round.

Rep this round once.

Next round: Knit using DP.

Next round: Purl using DP.

Next round: Knit using DP.

Next round: Purl using DP. Break off both shades.

Work 3 rounds purple stocking stitch, then purl one round using pale purple.

Break off pale purple and join in DP and PP.

Next round: K3 DP, *k3 PP, rep from * to end of round.

Rep this round once.

Next round: K3 PP, *k3 DP, rep from * to end of round.

Rep this round once.

Next round: K3 DP, *k3 PP, rep from * to end of round.

Rep this round once.

Next round: Knit using DP.

Next round: Purl using DP.

Next round: Knit using DP.

Next round: Purl using DP.

Crown Shaping

Change to pale purple DK (8 ply).

Next round: *K7, k2tog, rep from * to end of round.

Next round: Knit.

Next round: *K6, k2tog, rep from * to end of round.

Next round: Knit.

Next round: *K5, k2tog, rep from * to end of round.

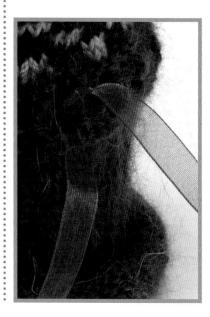

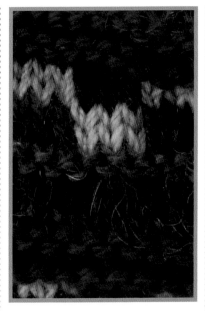

Fasten off.
Starting at the end with the sl st and dtr, roll up the rose, securing it with small stitches at the base. Stitch the roses around the feathers, securely to the crown. Sew in any loose ends.

Thread the ribbon through the eyelet holes, then tie in a generous bow.

Continue decreasing in this manner until the round k2tog all round has been worked.
Break off yarn, thread through rem sts, pull up tightly and fasten off. Sew in all ends on wrong side.

Feather Bases

Make 3 feather bases, 1 cream, 1 pale purple and 1 bright pink using 4 mm double-pointed knitting needles. Working backwards and forwards in rows, cast on 8 sts. Work 16 rows. Cast off.

Finishing Off Wrap firmly around the base of the feathers from the cast on end, rolling the knitted piece around the base of the feather. Stitch firmly to the centre of the hat, ensuring that they stand upright. Sew in any loose ends.

Crochet Roses

Make 3 in total, 1 using pale purple, 1 bright pink and 1 cream.
Using 3 mm crochet hook, make 48ch. Turn and miss 4ch, dtr into next 43 htr into last ch.
Next row: 3ch, 3tr into each dtr, to last 2 sts, 1 dbl, sl into last tr.

Bluebells Cockleshells

I love blue and wanted to use up lots of odds and ends of yarn that I had and this hat evolved as a result. This is an excellent project for using up half balls of yarn. To link it together I have used feather and fan stitch.

Size
To fit 18 months to 2 years

Materials
25 g DK (8 ply) of each of the following: pale blue, French blue, mid blue and bright blue
Small amounts of 4 ply in the following colours: bright blue, pale blue, navy, green

4 mm double-pointed knitting needles
2.25 mm double-pointed knitting needles
Wool needle

Butterfly

Three butterflies adorn this hat. A row of bobbles below the ribbed band giving the hat a very natty feel. Vary the colours according to your child's favourite.

Size

To fit 18 months to 2 years

Materials

1 x 50 g ball purple DK (8 ply)
1 x 50 g ball cream flecked
    DK (8 ply)
1 x 50 g ball variegated pink,
    aqua and orange DK (8 ply)
Small amounts of purple and
    pink 4 ply for the butterflies

4 mm double-pointed knitting
    needles
2 mm double-pointed
    knitting needles
Wool needle

Abbreviations

Mb (make bobble). To make a bobble k1, p1, k1, p1, k1 into the same st, turn, purl, turn, knit, turn, purl, turn, knit sl1, k1 *psso, k1, rep from * until 1 st rem).

Wrap: Bring yarn to front, slip next st from left to right needle, take yarn to back of work, return st back to left-hand needle. This prevents holes in the work when turning.

Using 4 mm double-pointed knitting needles and variegated yarn, cast on 95 sts (32, 31, 32). Knit 1 round.

Round 2: K2, *mb, k5, rep from * to last 2 sts, k3.

Round 3: Knit, decrease 5 sts evenly on this round: 2 sts on first needle, 1 st on second needle and 2 sts on third needle.

Break off variegated yarn, join in purple yarn.

Work 15 rounds k1, p1 rib.

Next round: Knit using purple.

Next round: Purl using variegated yarn.

Next round: Knit using variegated yarn.

Break off variegated yarn and join in cream flecked yarn and work 6 rounds as follows:

Round 1: *K1 cream, k2 purple, repeat from * to end of round.

Round 2: *K2 cream, k1 purple, repeat from * to end of round.

Round 3: As round 2.

Rounds 4-6: Repeat rounds 1-3.

Round 7: Purl using variegated yarn.

Round 8: Knit using variegated yarn.

Work 17 rounds st st in cream flecked without shaping.

Round 26: Purl using variegated yarn.

Round 27: Knit using variegated yarn.

Round 28: Knit using variegated yarn.

Round 29: Purl using variegated yarn.

Crown Shaping

Worked in alternating rounds of purple and variegated yarn.

Next round: *K7, k2tog, rep from * to end of round.

Next round: Knit.

Next round: *K6, k2tog, rep from * to end of round.

Next round: Knit.

Next round: *K5, k2tog, rep from * to end of round.

Continue decreasing in this manner until the round k2tog all round has been worked.

Break off yarn, thread through rem sts, pull up tightly and fasten off. Sew in all ends carefully on wrong side.

Butterfly

Using 2 mm double-pointed knitting needles and 4-ply yarn, cast on 12 sts.

Lower Wing

Row 1: (right side) K2, (p2, k1) 3 times, k1.
Row 2: K1, (p1, k2) 3 times, p1, k1.
Row 3: K2, (p2 tog, k1) 3 times, k1 (9 sts).
Row 4: K1, (p1, k1) 4 times.
Row 5: K1, sl2, k1, psso, p1, sl2, k1, psso, k1 (5 sts).
Row 6: K1, (p1, k1) twice.
Row 7: K1, sl2, k1, psso, k1 (3 sts).
Break off yarn, leave sts on a spare needle. Make 2 lower wings for each butterfly.

Upper Wing

Using 2 mm double-pointed knitting needles and 4-ply yarn, cast on 12 sts.
Row 1: (right side) K2, (p2, k1) 3 times, k1.
Row 2: K1, (p1, k2) 3 times, p1, k1.
Repeat rows 1 and 2 once.
Row 5: K2, (p2tog, k1) 3 times, k1 (9 sts).
Row 6: K1, (k1, p1) 4 times.
Row 7: K2, (p1, k1) 3 times, k1.
Row 8: As row 6.
Row 9: K1, sl2, k1, psso, p1, sl2, k1, psso, k1 (5 sts).
Row 10: K1 (p1, k1) twice.
Row 11: K1, sl2, k1, psso, k1 (3 sts).
Break off yarn; leave sts on a spare needle.
Make 2 upper wings for each butterfly.

Body

Using 2 mm double-pointed knitting needles and 4-ply yarn, cast on 6 sts.
Cast off knitwise.

To Make Up Join wings right sides together, line up the pair of upper wings and the pair of lower wings on 2 needles, and then use the 3rd needle to cast them off together knitwise. Press wings lightly. Stitch body to the top of the wings and use the yarn ends to make antennae. Make 3 butterflies in different shades.

To Finish

Stitch the butterflies to the sides of the hat at even intervals. Add more if you like, or use slightly thicker yarn to make them bigger.

Bobble

Using 2.25 mm knitting needles and purple, cast on 12 sts.
Row 1: Knit.
Row 2: P10, wrap.
Row 3: K8, wrap.
Row 4: P6, wrap.
Row 5: K4, wrap.
Row 6: Purl.
Rep these 6 rows another 4 times.
Cast off.
With right sides together sew side seam half way. Turn right side out and stuff firmly. Sew the rest of the seam and then run a gathering thread around the cast on edge.

Pull up firmly and fasten off. Do the same with the other end. Make sure you have sufficient filling and have made a firm ball. Stitch firmly to the top of the crown.

Polka Dots

This is a simple beanie, which is suitable for a boy or girl. If making for a boy, just omit the ribbon bow. The beanie is topped with red and white knitted balls and I-Cords. For a plainer look you could leave these off.

Size
To fit 2-3 years

Materials

2 x 50 g balls of red DK (8 ply)
1 x 50 g ball of white DK (8 ply)
1 m x 1 cm-wide white velvet
    ribbon

4 mm double-pointed
    knitting needles
2.75mm double-pointed
    knitting needles
Wool needle
Polyester fibre filling

Abbreviations

Wrap: bring yarn to front, slip next st from left to right needle, take yarn to back of work, return st to left-hand needle. This prevents holes in the work when turning.

Mb (make bobble): K1, p1, k1, p1, k1 into same st, turn, purl, turn, knit, turn, purl, turn, knit, sl1, k1 *psso, k1, rep from * until 1 st rem

Knitted Balls

Make two red-and-white striped balls and one red ball.

Using 2.75 mm knitting needles and red, cast on 12 sts.

Row 1: Knit.

Row 2: P10, wrap.

Row 3: Using white, k8, wrap.

Row 4: Using white, p6, wrap.

Row 5: Using red, k4, wrap.

Row 6: Using red, purl.

Rep these 6 rows another 4 times. Cast off.

With right sides together sew side seam half way. Turn right side out and stuff firmly. Sew the remainder of the seam and then run a gathering thread around the cast-on edge. Pull up firmly and fasten off. Do the same with the other end.

To make the red ball, leave out the white stripes.

I-Cords

Make 3 white and 3 red I-Cords. Using 2.75 mm double-pointed knitting needles and red, cast on 3 sts.

Knit the stitches, slide them to the end of the needle, pull the yarn firmly behind and knit the stitches again, continuing in this manner until each cord is 6 cm long. K2tog, psso. Fasten off.

Hat

Using 3.75 mm double-pointed knitting needles and red cast on 92 sts (30, 32, 30).

Work 32 rounds in k2, p2 rib.

Work 1 round in st st, dec 2 sts.

Work 2 more rounds.

Next round: Purl.

Eyelet round: K1, *yrn twice, k2tog, rep from * to end of round.

Next round: Knit dropping the second loop of the yrn twice off the needle as you knit.

Next round: Purl.

Next round: Purl.

Work 2 rounds st st.

**Bobble round: Join in white.

*k2, mb in white, rep from * ending round with k2.

Work 4 rounds st st in red.***

Rep from ** to *** another 3 times.

Crown Shaping

Round 1: *K7, k2tog, rep from * to end.

Round 2 and even rounds: Knit.

Round 3: *K6, k2tog, rep from * to end.

Round 5: *K5, k2tog, rep from * to end.

Keeping pattern of decreases continue in this manner until the round k1, k2tog has been worked. Break off yarn. Thread through rem sts, pull up tight and fasten off.

To Make Up

Sew in all ends. Attach knitted balls and I-Cords to the top of the hat. Turn up brim. Thread ribbon through eyelet holes and tie in a bow.

Chasing Rainbows

This bright and colourful beanie looks more complicated than it actually is. Made up of horizontal and vertical stripes, it also features decorative fancy bobbles and top knot flourishes.

Size
To fit 12-18 months

Materials

1 x 50 g ball purple DK (8 ply)
1 x 50 g ball bright pink DK (8 ply)
Small amounts of DK (8 ply) in bright green, orange, red bright blue and pale pink

4 mm double-pointed knitting needles
3 mm double-pointed knitting needles
Wool needle

Abbreviation

Mb (make bobble): k1, p1, k1, p1, k1 into same st, turn, purl, turn, knit, turn, purl, turn, sl1, k1 *psso, k1, rep from * until 1 st rems.

Using 4 mm double-pointed knitting needles and purple, cast on 92 sts (30, 32, 30). Join into a ring being careful not to twist the stitches.

Work 2 rounds k2, p2 rib.

Next round: Join in bright pink. *k2 pink, p2 purple, rep from * to end of round.

Rep this round another 13 times. Break off bright pink.

Next round: Knit using purple and decreasing 2 sts on second needle.

Next round: Purl.

Next round: Knit.

Next round: Purl.

Next round: Knit. Break off purple and fasten in bright pink. Knit 2 rounds.

Bobble round: Using bright pink *k4, mb, rep from * to end of round.

Next round: Knit.

Next round: Purl.

Next round: Knit using green.

Next round: Purl using green.

Next round: Knit using green.

Next round: Purl using green.

Next round: Knit using blue.

Next round: Purl using blue.

Next round: Knit using blue.

Next round: Purl using blue.

Next round: Knit using orange.

Next round: Purl using orange.

Next round: Knit using orange.

Next round: Purl using orange.

Next round: Knit using red.

Next round: Purl using red.

Next round: Knit using red.

Next round: Purl using red.

Next round: Knit using bright pink.

Next round: Purl using bright pink.

Next 2 rounds: Knit using bright pink.

Bobble round: Using bright pink *k4, mb, rep from * to end of round.

Next round: Knit using bright pink.

Next round: Purl using bright pink.

Next round: Knit using bright pink.

Crown Shaping

Work alternating rounds of bright pink and purple until all decreases have been worked.

Next round: *K7, k2tog, rep from * to end of round.

Next round: Knit.

Next round: *K6, k2tog, rep from * to end of round.

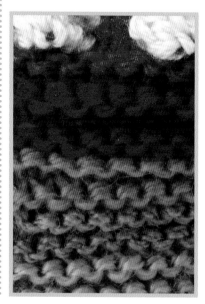

Next round: Knit.
Next round: *K5, k2tog, rep from * to end of round.
Continue in this manner until the round k2tog all round has been worked.
Break off yarn, thread through rem sts, pull up tightly and fasten off. Darn in all ends carefully on wrong side.

I-Cord Knots

Make 1 x green 14 cm, 1 x orange 10 cm, and 1 x bright pink 9 cm. Using two 3 mm double-pointed needles cast on 3 sts.
Row 1: Knit. Slide sts to other end of needle and pull yarn firmly behind. Do not turn work.
Repeat from * until I-Cord is desired length.
Next row: Sl1, k2tog, psso. Fasten off.

I-Cord Loops

Using 3 mm double-pointed needles cast on 3 sts and knit an I-Cord 9 cm long. Sl1, k2tog, psso. Break off yarn and draw through rem st. Fasten off neatly. Make desired loops in different sizes. Make 3 in total, 1 blue, 1 pale pink, 1 red.

To finish Stitch firmly in place on the crown. Sew a loop between each knotted I-Cord to make a symmetrical arrangement.

Blue Top Knot

This jolly bobbly hat is a great hat for boys and girls alike and is not too difficult to knit. The bobbles are knitted into the hat fabric and the colourful balls are knitted separately and attached at the end. Use any colourscheme you like.

Size
To fit 2-4 years

Materials
2 x 50 g balls bright blue DK (8 ply)
1 x 50 g ball cream DK (8 ply)
Small amounts bright green and aqua DK (8 ply)
4 mm double-pointed knitting needles

2.75 mm double-pointed knitting needles
Polyester fibre filling
Wool needle

Abbreviations

Mb (make bobble): K1, p1, k1, p1, k1 into same st, turn, purl, turn, knit, turn, purl, turn, knit sl1, k1 *psso, k1, rep from * until 1 st rem).

Wrap: Bring yarn to front, slip next st from left to right needle, take yarn to back of work, return st back to left-hand needle. This prevents holes in the work when turning.

Hat

Using 4 mm double-pointed knitting needles and bright blue DK (8 ply), cast on 92 (102) sts (30, 32, 30 / 34, 34, 34 sts). Join into a ring being careful not to twist the sts.

Work 32 rounds k2, k2 rib.

Next round: Knit, dec 2 sts evenly on this round (90/100) sts.

Work 2 rounds st st.

**Bobble round: Using cream *k2, mb, rep from * ending round with k2.

Work 4 rounds st st in blue.*
Rep from ** to * another 3 times.
Work another 2 rounds st st.

Crown Shaping

Next round: Using blue *K7 (8), k2tog, rep from * to end of round.
Next round: Knit.
Next round: *K6 (7), k2tog, rep from * to end of round.
Next round: Knit.
Next round: * K5 (6), k2tog, rep from * to end of round.
Continue decreasing in this manner until the round k2tog all round has been worked.
Break off yarn, thread through rem sts, pull up tightly and fasten off.

Sew in all ends carefully on the wrong side.

Knitted Balls

Make 1 white, 1 green, 1 aqua and 1 bright blue. Using 2.75 mm knitting needles and DK (8 ply), cast on 12 sts.
Row 1: Knit.
Row 2: P10, wrap.
Row 3: K8, wrap.
Row 4: P6, wrap.
Row 5: K4, wrap.
Row 6: Purl.
Rep these 6 rows another 4 times.
Cast off.
With right sides together sew side seam half way. Turn right side out and stuff firmly. Sew the remainder of the seam and then run a gathering thread around the cast-on edge. Pull up firmly and

fasten off. Do the same at the other end. Mould into a firm round ball.

I-Cords

Make 4 I-Cords each 15 cm long to match the knitted balls.
Using 2.75 mm double-pointed needles cast on 3 sts.
Knit the first row, slide them to the end of the needle, pull the yarn firmly behind and knit the stitches again, continuing in this manner until length is complete.
K2tog, psso. Fasten off.

To Make Up

Stitch 4 balls to the crown of the hat and the 4 I-Cords inbetween ensuring the colours alternate.
Turn up the ribbed brim.

Cherry Ripe

This delightful cherry-topped hat will brighten up any cold winter's day. Knit as many or as few cherries as you like. For a simple effect a single cherry on top would look equally as beautiful but for a more funky effect add the full bunch of 12; it's worth the extra time.

Size

To fit 18 months to 2 years

Materials

1 x 50 g ball cream DK (8 ply)
1 x 50 g ball variegated pink, red and orange DK (8 ply)
Small amounts of red and green DK (8 ply)
25 g red 4 ply for cherries
4 mm double-pointed knitting needles
2 mm knitting needles
2.25 mm double-pointed knitting needles
3 mm crochet hook
Polyester fibre filling
Wool needle

Crown Shaping

Work in alternating stripes of 1 round cream and 1 round variegated pink, red and orange.

Next round: *K7, k2tog, rep from * to end of round.

Next round: Knit.

Next round: *K6, k2tog, rep from * to end of round.

Next round: Knit.

Next round:* K5, k2tog, rep from * to end of round.

Continue decreasing in this manner until the round k2tog all round has been worked.

Break off yarn, thread through rem sts, pull up tightly and fasten off. Sew in all ends carefully on wrong side.

Abbreviation

Wrap: Bring yarn to front, slip next st from left to right needle, take yarn to back of work, return st to left-hand needle. This prevents holes in the work when turning.

Using 4 mm double-pointed knitting needles and variegated pink, red and orange, cast on 92 sts (30, 32, 30). Join into a ring being careful not to twist the stitches.

Work 32 rounds k2, p2 rib. Break off variegated yarn and join in cream.

Work 2 rounds st st, decreasing 2 sts evenly on first round.

Next round: Purl.

Next round: Knit.

Colour Band

Next round: Join in red and green *k3 green, k3 red, k3 cream, rep from * to end of round.
Rep this round once.

Next round: *K3 cream, k3 green. k3 red, rep from * to end of round.
Rep this round once.

Next round: *K3 green, k3 red, k3 cream, rep from * to end of round.
Rep this round once. Break off red and green yarn. Join in cream.

Next round: Knit.

Next round: Purl.

Work another 10 rounds st st in.

Next round: Purl.

Next round: Knit.

Next round: Knit using green.

Next round: Knit using red.

Next round: Knit using green.

Next round: Knit using cream.

Next round: Purl using cream.

Row 1: *Knit, do not turn work, pull sts to the other end of needle, pull yarn firmly behind. Rep from * until I-Cord is the right length. Now work in rows.

Row 2: K1, yfd, k1, yfd, k1.

Row 3 and all odd rows: Knit. First and last st, purl all other sts.

Row 4: K2, yfd, k1, yfd, k2.

Row 6: K3, yfd, k1, yfd, k3.

Row 8: K4, yfd, k1, yfd, k4.

Row 10: K5, yfd, k1, yfd, k5.

Row 12: Sl1, k1, psso, k9, k2tog.

Row 14: Sl1, k1, psso, k7, k2tog.

Row 16: Sl1, k1, psso, k5, k2tog.

Row 18: Sl1, k1, psso, k3, k2tog.

Row 20: Sl1, k1, psso, k1, k2tog.

Row 22: Sl2, k1, psso, fasten off.

Cherries

Using 2 mm needles and red 4 ply, cast on 12 sts.

Row 1: Knit.

Row 2: P10, wrap.

Row 3: K8, wrap.

Row 4: P6, wrap.

Row 5: K4, wrap.

Row 6: Purl.

Rep these 6 rows another 4 times. Cast off.

With right sides together sew side seam half way. Turn right side out and stuff firmly. Sew the rest of the seam and then run a gathering thread around the cast on edge. Pull up firmly and fasten off. Do the same with the other end. Make sure you have sufficient filling and each ball is round and firm. Make 12.

Stems

Using a 3 mm crochet hook make 20ch. Fasten off. Fold in half and fasten a cherry to each end. Attach the cherries to the crown of the hat.

I-Cord Leaves

Make 10.

Using 2 x 2.25mm double-pointed knitting needles, and green cast on 3 sts. Work an I-Cord for 3 cm.

Strawberries and Cream

Cheer up a wintery day with this vibrant, fruity beanie. Although the strawberries look tricky, the beads are threaded onto the yarn first, rather than embroidered on later. Make the hat first and set aside until the leaves and strawberries are complete.

Size

To fit 18 months to 2 years

Materials

1 x 50 g cream ball DK (8 ply)
1 x 50 g ball red DK (8 ply)
1 x 50 g ball multi-colour red-and- pink DK (8 ply)
1 x 50 g ball bright green DK (8 ply)
Small amount red 4 ply
Small amount bright green 4 ply
3.75 mm double-pointed knitting needles
2.75 mm double-pointed knitting needles
2 mm double-pointed knitting needles
2 packets Maria George red glass beads, size 8/0
Needle for threading beads on to 4-ply yarn
Wool needle
Polyester fibre filling

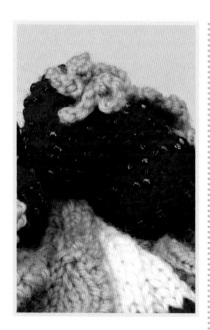

Abbreviations

B1: Bring yarn to the front, slip the next st purlwise, slide bead along yarn so that it sits firmly against the knitted fabric, take yarn to back of work, ready to knit next st.
Mb (make bobble): K1, p1, k1, p1, k1 into same st, turn, purl, turn, knit, turn, purl, turn, sl1, k1 *psso, k1, rep from * until 1 st rems.

Hat

Using 3.75 mm double-pointed knitting needles and multi-colour red and pink DK (8 ply), cast on 90 sts (30, 30, 30).
Work 10 rounds of st st for brim. Break off multi-colour yarn and join in red 8 ply.
Work 14 rounds k1, p1, rib. Rejoin multi-colour yarn.

Round 25: Knit using multi-colour.
Round 26: Purl using multi-colour.
Round 27: Knit using multi-colour.
Bobble round: Join in cream DK (8 ply). Using multi-colour *k4, mb, rep from * to end of round. Work bobbles in cream.
Rounds 29 and 30: Knit using multi-colour.
Round 31: Purl using multi-colour. Join in red 8 ply.
Using red work 6 rounds st st.
Round 38: Purl using multi-colour.
Rounds 39 and 40: Knit using multi-colour. Join in cream.
Bobble round: Using multi-colour *k4, mb (using cream), rep from * to end of round. **Rounds 42 and 43**: Knit using multi-colour.
Round 44: Purl using multi-colour. Using red DK (8 ply) work 4 rounds st st.

Crown Shaping

Work rem of hat in cream DK (8 ply).
Round 1: *K7, k2tog, rep from * to end.
Round 2 and all even rounds: Knit.
Round 3: *K6, k2tog, rep from * to end.
Round 5: *K5, k2tog, rep from * to end.
Keeping pattern of decreases continue in this manner until the round k1, k2tog has been worked. Break off yarn. Thread through rem sts, pull up tight and fasten off.

Strawberries

Thread all the beads onto the 4 ply red yarn. Make 5.

Berry Body

Make one back and one front.
Using 2 mm double-pointed knitting needles and red 4 ply, cast on 3 sts.
Row 1: (wrong side) Inc in first st, p1, inc in last st (5 sts).
Row 2: (K1, b1) twice, k1.
Row 3: Inc in first st, p3, inc in last st (7 st).
Rows 4, 6 and 8: (K1, b1) to last st, k1.
Row 5: Inc in first st, p5, inc in last st (9 sts).
Row 7: Inc in first st, p7, inc in last st (11 sts).
Rows 9, 11, 13 and 15: K1, p9, k1.
Rows 10 and 14: K2, (b1, k1) to last st, k1.

Rows 12 and 16: (K1, b1) to last st, k1.

Rows 17: Sl1, K1 psso, (b1, k1) to last 3 sts, b1, k2tog (9 sts).

Rows 18: K1, p7, k1.

Cast off.

Calyx

Using 2 mm double-pointed knitting needles and bright green 4 ply, cast on 8 sts.

Row 1: (wrong side) Cast off 5 sts, k2 (3 sts).

Row 2: K3, turn, cast on 5 sts (8 sts).

Repeat rows 1 and 2 four times. Cast off.

To Make Up Sew strawberry right

sides together, leaving top open. Turn right side out. Stuff firmly with polyester fibre filling. Roll the calyx and secure along the cast-off edge. Sew to the top of the strawberry. Manipulate to a good shape.

Leaves

(Make 10)

Using 2.75 mm double-pointed knitting needles and bright green DK (8 ply), cast on 8 sts, cast off 7 sts, (1 st).

Row 1: (right side) K1, inc, k1.

Row 2: Purl.

Row 3: K1, m1, k1, m1, k1.

Row 4 and all even rows: Knit first and last st and purl rem sts.

Row 5: K2, m1, k1, m1, k2.

Row 7: K3, m1, k1, m1, k3.

Row 9: K4, m1, k1, m1, k4.

Row 11: K5, m1, k1, m1, K5.

Row 13: Knit.

Row 15: Knit.

Row 17: K5, sl2, k1, psso, k5.

Row 19: K4, sl2, k1, psso, k4.

Row 21: K3, sl2, k1, psso, k3.

Row 23: K2, sl2, k1, psso, k2.

Rows 24 and 26: Purl.

Row 25: K1, sl2, k1, psso, k1 (3 sts).

Row 27: K1, sl2, psso, fasten off.

Press leaves to flatten into shape.

To Make Up

Attach the leaves fanning out from the centre of the top of the hat and then stitch the strawberries firmly on the top. Sew in all ends.

Twist and Twirl

Turn heads with this twizzling number. Perfect for boys or girls just change your colourscheme to suit. The crown decorations are added when the hat is complete. Everything else is incorporated into the knitting as you go. This pattern provides a good opportunity to use up small amounts of left-over yarn.

Size
To fit 18 months to 2 years

Materials
1 x 50 g ball red DK (8 ply)
1 x 50 g ball navy DK (8 ply)
Small amounts DK (8 ply) in
    eight bright colours
5 x 4 mm double-pointed
    knitting needles

3 mm double-pointed knitting
    needles
Wool needle
Polyester fibre filling

Abbreviations

Mb (make bobble) K1, p1, k1, p1, k1 into same stitch (5 sts), turn, purl, turn, knit, turn, purl, turn, knit. Pass, second st, on right-hand needle over first st. Repeat until 1 st remains on right-hand needle.

Kt (knitted twirl): With contrast colour and spare double-pointed knitting needle knit into next st and cast on 15 sts. Knit 2 rows on these sts in contrast colour. Cast off 15 sts.

Using 4 mm double-pointed knitting needles and red DK (8 ply), cast on 90 sts onto 3 needles. Join into a ring being careful not to twist sts.

Work 32 rounds k1, p1 rib.

Change to navy blue DK (8 ply) and work 1 round knit.

Next round: Purl.
Next round: Knit.
Next round: Purl.
Next round: Knit.
Next round: *K8, (using a different colour for each twirl), kt, rep from * to end of round.

Work another 2 rounds (each round knit) in navy blue.

Next round: Purl.
Next round: Knit.
Next round: Purl.
Next round: Knit.
Next round: Knit.

Bobble round: Using bright green *k4, mb, rep from * ending round with mb.

Knit 2 rounds knit navy blue.

Next round: Purl.
Next round: Knit.
Next round: *K8, (using a different colour for each twirl), kt, rep from * to end of round.

Knit 2 rounds navy blue.

Next round: Purl.
Next round: Knit.
Next round: Purl.
Next round: Knit.

Crown Shaping

Change to red DK (8 ply).

Next round: *K7, k2tog, rep from * to end of round.
Next round: Knit.
Next round: *K6, k2tog, rep from * to end of round.
Next round: Knit.
Next round: *K5, k2tog, rep from * to end of round.

Continue decreasing in this

manner until the round k2tog all round has been worked.

Break off yarn, thread through rem sts, pull up tightly and fasten off. Sew in all ends on wrong side.

Knitted Balls

Make 3 in different colours.

Using 3 mm knitting needles, cast on 12 sts. Work backwards and forwards in rows.

Row 1: K12.
Row 2: P10, wrap 1, turn.
Row 3: K8, wrap 1, turn.
Row 4: P6, wrap 1, turn.
Row 5: K4, wrap 1, turn.
Row 6: P to end.

Rep rows 1–6 four times, cast off.

To Make Up

Sew cast off and on ends together and stuff firmly to form a ball. Use either the knit or purl side. Sew firmly to crown of hat.

I-Cord Loops

Using 3 mm needles and 8 ply, cast on 3 sts, knit one row, do not turn, *slide sts to other end of needle and pull yarn firmly behind, knit next row. Repeat from * until cord is desired length. Sl1, k2tog, psso, fasten off.

Make 6 I-Cords each 10 cm long. Join into a loop by stitching ends together. Sew firmly inbetween knitted balls on crown.

Loopy Hat

This cheerful loopy hat knitted in varying shades of blue is perfect for keeping out chills and brightening up a winter's day. Make I-Cord loops first, then set them aside until they're knitted into the main body of the hat.

Size
To fit 12-18 months

Materials
Several shades of blue DK (8 ply)
4 mm double-pointed knitting
   needles
3.5 mm crochet hook
Wool needle

Stitch holders
Polyester fibre filling

Make the loops and balls first.

I-Cord Loops

Using double-pointed needles and an oddment of yarn, cast on 3 sts. Knit an I-Cord 9cm long.

Row 1: *Knit, do not turn work, pull sts to the other end of needle, pull yarn firmly behind. Rep from * until I-Cord is the right length. Sl1, k2tog, psso and leave rem st on stitch holder.
Make 30.

Crochet Balls

With crochet hook, make 4ch and form into a loop.

Round 1: Work 6dc into the loop.

Round 2: *Work 2dc into first, 1dc into next st. Rep from * to end of round. Join with sl st.

Rounds 3 and 4: Work 1dc into each st. Stuff the ball at this stage or the gap will be too small.

Round 5: *1dc into first st, miss 1 st, rep from * to end. Break off yarn. Run thread through stitches, pull up tightly and fasten off. Make sure ball is firmly stuffed.
Make 5.

Hat

Using 3.75 mm double-pointed knitting needles cast on 80 sts evenly on 3 needles (26, 28, 26). Work in k2, p2 rib for 30 rows. Change to st st and work 10 rounds, changing colours as desired.

Loop round 1: K4, *place loop by placing end of I-Cord in front of rems st and pass over, so that the I-Cord becomes a loop. Then place in front of main body of knitting and knit together with the next st), k7, rep from * to end of round adding in a different coloured loop each time.

Work another 6 rounds st st.

Loop round: K7, *place loop by placing end of I-Cord in front of rem st and pass over, so that the I-Cord becomes a loop. Then place in front of main body of knitting and knit together with the next st), k7, rep from * to end of round adding in a different coloured loop each time.

Knit 4 rounds st st.

Loop round: Work as loop round 1. Work 3 rounds st st.

Crown Shaping

Round 1: *K6, k2tog , rep from * to end.

Round 2 and all even rounds: Knit.

Round 3: *K5, k2tog, rep from * to end.

Round 5: *K4, k2tog, rep from * to end.

Continue decreasing in this manner until the round k1, k2tog has been worked.

Break off yarn, Thread through rem sts, pull up tightly and fasten off.

Sew in all ends. Stitch the crocheted balls securely to the top of the hat. Fold up brim.

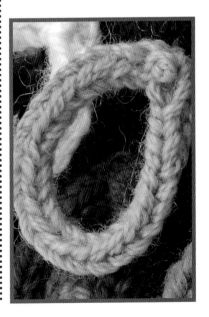

Carnival

Keep out the winter chills and put a smile on the face of the lucky child who receives this cheerful hat. This hat is very textural in design and features bobbles, knitted-in twists and triangular shapes, and a striped ribbed band. It's not a beginner's project but the knitting is exciting and the end result very worthwhile.

Size
To fit 18 months to 2 years

Materials
1 x 50 g ball red DK (8 ply)
1 x 50 g ball white DK (8 ply)
1 x 50 g ball navy DK (8 ply)
1 x 50 g ball medium blue DK (8 ply)
1 x 50 g ball light blue DK (8 ply)

3 x 3.75 mm double-pointed knitting needles
3.5 mm crochet hook
1 spare needle
Wool needle

Abbreviation

Mb (make bobble) as follows: k1, p1, k1, p1, k1 into same st, turn, purl, turn, knit, turn purl, turn, sl1, k1 *psso, k1, rep from * until 1 st rems.

Triangle Flaps

Cast on 9 stitches; divide evenly on 3 needles and join into a circle, being careful not to twist the stitches. (You will be left with live stitches for grafting.)

Round 1: Knit.
Round 2: *K1, inc in next st, k1, rep from * to end.
Rounds 3 and 4: Knit.
Round 5: * K1, inc in next 2 sts, k1, rep from * to end.
Rounds 6 and 7: Knit.
Round 8: *K1, inc in next st, rep

from * to end.
Rounds 9 and 10: Knit.
Round 11: Knit to last 2 sts, k2tog.
Round 12: Divide sts evenly on to two needles. Holding sts parallel, k2tog all across. Graft live sts together at the cast-on edge or if it is awkward you could run a thread through the live sts, pull up tightly and fasten off.

Make 4 light blue, 4 medium blue and 1 red triangle. Set aside on spare needle.

Hat

Begin at lower edge.
Using 3.75 mm double-pointed needles and navy, cast on 90 sts evenly on 3 needles (30, 30, 30). Join into a circle, being careful not to twist the stitches.
Work 10 rows st st for rolled brim.

Join in white and work in k1, p1 rib alternating the colours. Begin with k1 in navy, p1 white. Work 10 rows. Break of navy and white and join in medium blue.
Work 2 rounds st st.
Attach triangles by holding spare needle in front of work and knitting the stitches from the triangle together with the hat stitches alternating light blue and medium blue triangles all the way around and ending with one red triangle. Work sequence as follows as you add each triangle: *k2tog, k3, k2tog, k4, k2tog place next triangle and continue from * until all triangles are added.
Work another 3 rounds of medium blue st st.

Next round: Knit using white.
Next round: Purl using white.
Next round: Knit using navy.
Next round: Purl using navy.
Knit 2 rounds red.
Bobble round: Using red *k4, mb, rep from * to end of round.
Work another 2 rounds red in st st.
Next round: Knit using navy.
Next round: Purl using navy.
Next round: Knit using white.
Next round: Purl using white.
Work 4 rounds st st medium blue.

Twisted Cords

*Using white, cast on 15 sts into the first st of the round, cast off. St st 9 sts in mid blue. Work from *to * in navy. Work another 9 sts in mid blue in st st and work from *to* in red. Continue in this sequence, until the round is complete. There will be 9 twisted cords in total, 3 of each colour.

Work another 3 rounds medium blue.

Next round: Knit using navy.

Next round: Purl using navy.

Next round: Knit using white.

Next round: Purl using white.

Break off navy and join in red. Work 1 round red in st st.

Crown Shaping

Join in white. Work 1 round st st alternating red and white. Commence decrease for crown keeping continuity of red and white striped pattern.

Round 1: *K7, k2tog, rep from * to end.

Round 2 and even rounds: Knit.

Round 3: *K6, k2tog, rep from * to end.

Round 5: * K5, k2tog, rep from * to end.

Continue decreasing in this manner until the round K1, k2tog has been worked. Break off yarn. Thread through rem sts, pull up tight and fasten off.

I-Cord

Make 1 of each colour, 5 in total. Either pick up a stitch on top of the hat, cast on 2 more and then commence the I-Cord. Knitting the stitches, slide them to the end of the needle, pull the yarn firmly behind and knit the stitches again, continuing in this manner until each I-Cord is 7 cm long. Alternately, make the I cord separately and then sew them to the top of the hat.

Finishing

Sew in all ends. The hat should not need pressing as this will flatten the bobbles, however you might need to press the triangles.

Socks on The Washing Line

Indulge your passion for knitting sock and hats with this whimsical design. Tiny socks are strung on a washing line around the hat and one sock sits on top, surrounded by buttoned I-Cord loops. If you have knitted socks before, you will easily be able to manage these scaled-down versions.

Size
To fit 2-4 years

Materials

2 x 50 g balls of red DK (8-ply) wool
Small amount of 4-ply sock yarn in desired colour
Small amount of 4-ply red
15 small red buttons
3.75 mm double-pointed knitting needles

2 mm double-pointed knitting needles
Polyester fibre filling
Wool needle
Red sewing cotton
Sewing needle

Using 3.75 mm double-pointed knitting needles and red DK (8 ply), cast on 90 sts (30, 30, 30). Work 28 rounds in k1, p1 rib. Work 5 rounds in st st.
Round 1: Purl.
Work 12 rounds st st.
Round 14: Purl.
Work 5 rounds st st.
Round 20: Purl.

Crown Shaping
Round 1: *K7, k2tog, rep from * to end.
Round 2 and even rounds: Knit.
Round 3: *K6, k2tog, rep from * to end.
Round 5: *K5, k2tog, rep from * to end.
Keeping pattern of decreases continue in this manner until the round k1, k2tog has been worked.

Break off yarn. Thread through rem sts, pull up tight and fasten off.

I-Cord Washing Line
Using 2 mm double-pointed knitting needles make an I-Cord casting on 2 stitches.
Row 1: *Knit, do not turn work, pull sts to the other end of needle, pull yarn firmly behind. Rep from * until I-Cord is the right length. Sl1, k1, psso and fasten off. Ensure that it is long enough to fit loosely around the hat.

Socks
Using 2 mm double-pointed knitting needles and 4-ply sock yarn cast on 24 sts (8 on each needle).
Work 5 rounds k1, p1 rib.
Work 6 rounds st st.

Divide for Heel
Knit next 6 sts onto first needle, slip last 6 sts of third needle onto same needle (12 sts). (These sts will be worked backwards and forwards in rows).
Divide rem sts between 2 needles.
Row 1: Sl1, purl to end.
Row 2: *Sl1, k1, rep from * to end.
Rep these two rows twice more and then row 1 once more.

Turn Heel
K8, turn, p4, turn, k3, sl1, k1, psso, k1, turn, p4, p2tog, p1, turn, k5, sl1, k1, psso, k1, turn, cont in this manner until all heel sts have been worked onto one needle (8 sts).
Slip instep sts on to one needle.
Knit first 4 heel sts with first needle then second 4 heel sts with

second needle (4 heel sts on each needle and all instep sts on one needle).

Commencing at centre heel, k4, pick up 6 sts along side of heel, using next needle knit across instep sts, using next needle, pick up and k6 sts along other side of heel, knit rem 4 heel sts.

Shape In-step
Round 1: Knit.
Round 2: First needle, knit to last 3 sts, k2tog, k1. Second needle, knit. Third needle, k1, sl1, psso, knit to end.
Rep these two rounds until there are 6 sts left on first and third needles and 12 sts left on second needle. Work another 3 rounds without shaping.

Shape Toe
Round 1: Knit.
Round 2: First needle knit to last 3 sts, k2tog, k1. Second needle k1, sl1, k1, psso, knit to last 3 sts, k2tog, k1. Third needle, k1, sl1, k1, psso, knit to end.
Rep these two rounds until there are 3 sts left on first and third needles and 6 sts left on the second needle. Slip sts from the third needle onto the first needle and graft sts together.
Make 6.

I-Cord Loops
Using two double-pointed knitting needles and red 8 ply, cast on 3 sts and knit an I-Cord 9 cm long, following the instructions for the I-Cord Washing Line. Sl1, k2tog, psso, pass point of needle through the end of the I-Cord to form a loop and place this stitch on the right-hand needle, draw the first stitch over it and fasten off to create a loop. Sew the button in the centre of the join.

To Make Up
Catch the washing line to the hat at 5 points on the two purl rows with holding stitches. At each of these points attach a knitted sock, securing on the outside with a button. Make sure all the socks face the same direction. Lightly stuff one sock and stitch closed along the top of the ribbing. Stitch to the centre of the top of the hat. Sew the buttoned loops evenly around the top of the hat, securing through the buttons. Sew in all ends.

Blooming Gorgeous

I wanted the flowers on this hat to look like they were coming out of the crown. To make it extra special I have added a little watering can and a row of pink bobbles around the edge of the crown. The pleats are created by adding extra stitches and then pulling the carrying yarn very tightly behind the stitches being knitted. This is similar to the way old-fashioned tea cosies were created.

Size

To fit 2-4 years

Materials
1 x 50 g ball medium pink DK
   (8-ply) pure wool
1 x 50 g ball bright green DK
   (8-ply) pure wool
1 x 50 g ball mid green DK
   (8-ply) pure wool
1 x 50 g ball deep pink DK
   (8-ply) pure wool
Small amount pale pink DK
   (8-ply) pure wool

Small amount cream DK
   (8-ply) pure wool
Small amount variegated pink
   DK (8-ply) pure wool
Part ball, green cotton 4 ply
Pale green glass beads
Small piece cardboard
Polyester fibre filling
4 mm double-pointed knitting
   needles

3.25 mm double-pointed
   knitting needles
2 mm knitting needles
3 mm crochet hook
Wool needle
Beading needle
Sewing needle
Green sewing thread

Abbreviation

Mb (Make bobble): K1, p1, k1, p1, k1 into same st, turn, purl, turn, knit, turn, purl, turn, knit, sl1, k1 *psso, k1, rep from * until 1 st rems.

Using 4 mm double-pointed knitting needles and medium pink cast on 90 sts (30, 30, 30). Join into a ring, being careful not to twist sts.

Work 12 rounds k1, p1 rib.

Round 13: Inc in every sts (180 sts).

Next round: *K1, inc in next st, rep from * to end (270 sts).

Break off medium pink and join in bright green and deep pink.

Next round: *K9 green, k9 pink, (Pull the yarn not in use very firmly across the back of the work. This will cause the knitting to feel quite tight, this is correct. It will create the pleats) rep from * ending with k9 pink. Rep this round until work measures 14 cm from beg of rib.

Next round: * K2tog, k2tog, k1, k2tog twice, rep from * to end.

Next round: *K2tog, k1, k2tog, rep from * to end (90 sts).

Work 1 round deep pink st st.

Break off deep pink. Break off deep pink. Join in medium pink work 2 rounds st st.

Bobble round: Using medium pink *k4, mb, rep from * to end of round.

Work another 2 rounds st st in medium pink.

Crown shaping

Round 1: Using medium pink *k7, k2tog, rep from * to end.

Round 2 and all even rounds: Knit.

Round 3: *K6, k2tog, rep from * to end.

Round 5: *K5, k2tog, rep from * to end.

Continue decreasing in this manner until the round k1, k2tog has been worked. Break off yarn. Thread through rem sts, pull up tight and fasten off.

I-Cord Leaves

Using 3.25 mm double-pointed knitting needles, and bright green, cast on 3 sts and make a 2 cm I-Cord. Then

Row 1: Knit.

Row 2: Purl.

Row 3: K1, m1, k1 tbl, m1, k1.

Row 4 and all even rows: Knit first and last st, purl the sts inbetween.

Row 5: K2, m1, k1 tbl, m1, k2.

Row 7: K3, m1, k1 tbl, m1, k3.

Row 9: K4, m1, k1 tbl, m1, k4.

Row 11: K5, m1, k1 tbl, m1, k5.

Row 13: K5, sl2, k1, psso, k5.

Row 15: K4, sl2, k1, psso, k4.

Row 17: K3, sl2, k1, psso, k3.

Row 19: K2, sl2, k1, psso, k2.

Row 21: K1, sl2, k1, psso, k1.

Row 23: Sl2 sts, k1, psso.

Fasten off. Make 10 in total: 5 bright green and 5 mid green.

Watering Can

Using 2 mm knitting needles and green 4-ply cotton cast on 45 sts. Work 2 rows garter st.

Begin with a knit row, work 25 rows st st.

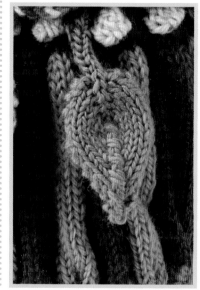

Work 2 rows garter st.
Begin with a purl row, work 3 rows st st.

Base Shaping
Row 1: (K3, k2tog) to end (36 sts).
Row 2 and even rows: Purl.
Row 3: (K2, k2tog) to end (27 sts).
Row 5: (K1, k2tog) to end (18 sts).
Row 7: (K2tog) to end (9 sts).
Break off yarn, pull up tightly and fasten off.
Oversew row ends together and turn right side out. Cut out a cardboard circle the same size as the base of the watering can and put in place.

Spout
Using 2 mm knitting needles and green 4-ply cotton cast on 8 sts.
Work 2 rows st st.
Row 1: Inc knitwise into firs st, knit to last 2 sts, inc into next st, k1 (10 sts).
Work 3 rows st st.
Repeat the last 4 rows 3 more times (16 sts).
Dec 1 st at each end of next and foll alt rows until 4 st rem. Cast off.
Beginning at the cast on edge, oversew the row ends together as far as the ends of the increases. Turn right side out and stuff very firmly. Sew the open ends to the side of the watering can with cast off edge, 4 rows above the base of the can. Add more stuffing, as needed.

Watering Can Rose
Using 2 mm knitting needles and green 4-ply cotton, cast on 12 sts.
Row 1: inc in every st (24 sts).
Beginning with a purl row, work 4 rows st st.
Next row: Knit.
Next row: Purl.
Beginning with a purl row work 3 rows st st.
Next row: (K1, k2tog) to end (16 sts).
Next row: (K2tog) to end (8 sts).
Break off yarn, pull up tightly and fasten off.
Oversew row ends together. Turn right side out and stuff firmly. Sew very firmly to the end of the spout.

Stitch green glass beads to the rose.

Handles
Make one I-Cord 6 cm long and one 12 cm long. Attach the 12 cm cord to the top of the watering can and the 6 cm cord to the back of the watering can to form handles. Stitch the watering can firmly to the top of the hat.

Roses
Using a 3 mm crochet hook, make 48ch. Turn, and miss 4ch, dtr into next 43ch, tr into last ch.
Next row: 3ch, 3 tr into each dtr, to last 2 sts, 1dbl, sl into last tr.
Fasten off.
Starting at the end with the sl st and dbl crochet, roll up the rose. Stitch securely at the base.

Make 6 in total, 2 bright pink, 2 variegated pink, and 2 cream. Attach to the hat around the watering can.

Flowers for the Watering Can

Using a 3 mm crochet hook and dark pink, make 4ch, join into a ring with a ss.

Round 1: (right side) 2ch, 9dc in ring with pale pink, ss to top of 2ch (10 sts).

Round 2: 5ch, 1tr in each of next 9dc, ss to top of 5ch. Fasten off. Make 3 in total. Use dark pink for the centre and pale pink for the outer petals.

To Make Up Sew in ends and form into a neat circular shape. Stitch the flowers to the opening at the top of the watering can.

To Make Up

Sew the watering can firmly to the centre of the crown. Surround the can with the five crocheted roses, stitching each firmly in place. Catch down the leaves between every two bobbles at the start of the crown shaping. Alternate the leaf colours if you have used different shades.

If you don't have a hat block, you can stuff your entire hat with polyester fibre filling to give it a round shape. This makes attaching decorations easier as you can see the work more easily.

The Tea Party

This hat is shaped like a cup cake with a little tea party on top. Complete with a tea pot, jam tarts and cream pies, and surrounded by pretty pink daises. This is a very feminine beanie. The basic hat is very quick to knit, but take your time with the decorations and your patience will pay off.

Size

To fit 18 months to 2 years

Materials

1 x 50 g ball pink variegated DK (8 ply)
1 x 50 g ball cream DK (8 ply)
Small amounts of 4 ply in pale pink, bright blue, fawn, crimson, white and cream
Stranded embroidery cotton in pale blue
Polyester fibre filling

Cardboard scrap
Chenille pipe cleaner
4 mm double-pointed knitting needles
2 mm knitting needles
3 mm crochet hook
Sewing needle
Wool needle

Using 4 mm double-pointed knitting needles and variegated pink 8 ply, cast on 90 sts (30, 30, 30). Join into a ring, being careful not to twist sts.

Work 34 rounds k1, p1 rib.

Break off pink and join in cream.

Next round: Purl.

Cont in st st, (every round knit) until work measures 19 cm from beg.

Crown Shaping

Round 1: *K7, k2tog, rep from * to end of round.

Round 2: Knit.

Round 3: *K6, k2tog, rep from * to end of round.

Round 4: Knit.

Round 5: *K5 k2tog, rep from * to end of round.

Continue decreasing in this

manner until the round k2tog all round has been worked.

Break off yarn, thread through rem sts, pull up tightly and fasten off. Sew in all ends carefully on wrong side.

Crochet Frill

With 3 mm crochet hook and cream 8 ply, insert hook into purl loop on the purl row at the top of the rib.

*Work 3ch, dc into next purl loop, rep from * all the way around hat finishing with a sl st into first st.

Teapot

Using 2 mm knitting needles and bright blue 4 ply, cast on 9 sts.

Row 1: Purl.

(Now work in stripes of 2 rows blue and 2 rows white until ***then con-

tinue in bright blue.)

Row 2: Inc into every st (18 sts). Purl 2 more rows.

Commencing with a purl row work 8 rows st st.

Row 13: *P1, p2tog, rep from * to end.***

Row 14: Purl.

Commencing with a purl row, st st 2 rows.

Row 17: P2tog to end (6 sts).

Row 18: Inc in every st (12 sts).

Break off yarn, thread through rem sts, pull up tightly and fasten off.

To Make Up Cut a cardboard base the size of a small coin. Because the teapot is so small it is easier to sew it up the right side out; just use very tiny stitches. Sew row ends together to the half-way point then insert the carboard coin in the base. Stuff the teapot firmly. Take a strand of blue 4 ply and attach it firmly to the top of the teapot just below the stitches you have pulled up tightly. Pull the yarn around these stitches to make a knob. Fasten off firmly. Continue stuffing the teapot until you have a firm round shape. Close seam.

Spout

Using 2 mm knitting needles and bright blue 4 ply, cast on 6 sts. Beg with a knit row, work 3 rows st st.

Row 4: P2, p2tog, p2.

Work another 3 rows st st.

Cast off.

Fold spout in half. Cut pipe cleaner to fit, bending sharp ends over. Stitch the seam closed, then sew the thinner end to the teapot, at the second blue stripe. Bending the spout into shape.

Handle

Using 2 mm knitting needles and bright blue 4 ply, make a 2-stitch I-Cord 3 cm long.

Row 1: *Knit, do not turn work, pull sts to the other end of needle, pull yarn firmly behind. Rep from * until I-Cord is the right length. Sl1, k1, psso and fasten off. Attach to teapot opposite spout.

Jam Tart

Using 2 mm knitting needles and crimson 4 ply, cast on 16 sts. Knit 1 row.

Row 2: P2tog all across.
Break off yarn, thread through rem sts, pull up tightly and fasten off. Fold in half and sew row ends together. Darn in ends and shape into a circle to make jam centre. Make 2.

Pastry casing

Using 2 mm knitting needles and fawn 4 ply, cast on 24 sts. Cast off. Sew row end together to form a ring. Make 2
Place jam centre in pastry casing and stitch into place.

Plate

Using 2 mm knitting needles and bright blue 4 ply, cast on 35 sts. Work 3 rows garter st.

Row 4: *P1, p2tog, rep from *to end.

Row 5: Knit.

Row 6: P2tog all across.
Break off yarn, thread through rem sts, pull up tightly and fasten off.

Carefully stitch row ends together forming a round shape. Sew in ends.
Place a jam tart on each plate and stitch into place.

Cream Pie

Using 2 mm knitting needles and two strands of fawn 4 ply, cast on 24 sts, cont with just 1 strand and knit 2 rows garter st.

Row 3: *K1, k2tog, rep from * to end.

Row 4: Purl.

Row 5: K2tog all across.
Break off yarn, thread through rem sts, pull up tightly and fasten off. Fold in half and sew row ends together. Sew in ends and shape into a circle.

Cream Top

Using 2 mm knitting needles and cream 4 ply, cast on 16 sts.

Row 1: Purl.

Row 2: * K1, inc in next st, rep from * to end (24 sts).
Commencing with a purl row, work 3 rows st st.

Row 6: *K1, k2tog, rep from * to end (16 sts).
Row 7: P2tog all across.
Break off yarn, thread through rem sts, pull up tightly and fasten off.

To Make Up Stitch row ends closed, then stuff with a little polyester fibre filling to make a round shape. Place piece on top of base and stitch into place enclosing all filling.
Make 2.

Flowers

Using 2 mm knitting needles and pale pink 4 ply, cast on 16 sts.
Knit 1 row.
Row 2: P2tog all across.
Break off yarn, thread through rem sts, pull up tightly and fasten off.
Fold in half and sew row ends

together. Darn in ends and shape into a circle.
Using blue embroidery cotton work a couple of small straight stitches in the centre of each flower and a bullion knot on top of the straight stitches. Make 10.

To Make Up

Firmly sew teapot to centre of crown and then sew the jam tarts and the cream pies around the teapot. Sew the 10 pink flowers at intervals around the hat.
Turn up the brim.

Blackberry Pie

What better way to keep your head warm in winter than to have your own blackberry pie to wear. It is complete with pie crust, ornamental knitted blackberries and leaves. It's a great hat for a budding chef or keen gardener.

Size
To fit 2–4 years

Materials

I x 50 g ball oatmeal DK (8-ply) wool

2 x 50 g balls, purple DK (8-ply) wool

Small amount green DK (8 ply) for leaves and calyx

Small amount of purple/pink 4-ply wool for berries and blackberry pie

Small amount of green 4-ply wool for berry and calyx

140 glass beads with a big enough hole to thread onto 4-ply yarn

4 mm double-pointed knitting needles

2 mm knitting needles

2.25 mm knitting needles

2.75 mm double-pointed knitting needles

3 mm crochet hook

Wool needle

Polyester fibre filling

Abbreviation

Mb (make bobble): K1, p1, k1, p1, k1 into same st, turn, purl, turn, knit, turn, purl, turn, sl1, k1, *psso, k1, rep from * until 1 st rems.

Using 4 mm double-pointed knitting needles and oatmeal DK (8-ply) wool, cast on 90 sts, 30 30 30. Join into a round being careful not to twist sts.

Work 30 rounds of k1, p1 rib. Break off oatmeal and join in purple.

Next round: Purl, dec 1 (89 sts).

Work in blackberry stitch until work measures 18 cm from cast on edge.

Blackberry stitch: These 8 rows form pattern:

Round 1: Knit.

Round 2: K1, *m5, k1, rep from * to end.

Round 3: Knit.

Round 4: K1, *sl2, yfd, p3tog, psso, k1, rep from * to end.

Round 5: Knit.

Round 6: K1, *k1, m5, k1, rep from * to end.

Round 7: Knit.

Round 8: K1, *k1, sl2, yfd, p3tog, psso, k1, rep from * to last st, k1.

Turn hat inside out to reveal right side of work.

Inc round: Knit using purple, inc 1 st. Break off purple. Join in oatmeal and knit 2 rounds.

Bobble round: Work in purple as follows: *K4, mb, rep from * ending round with mb.

Knit 2 rounds oatmeal.

Crown Shaping

Next round: *K7, k2tog, rep from * to end of round.

Next round: Knit.

Next round: *K6, k2tog, rep from * to end of round.

Next round: Knit.

Next round: *K5, k2tog, rep from * to end of round.

Continue decreasing in this manner until the round k2tog all round has been worked.

Break off yarn, thread through rem sts, pull up tightly and fasten off. Sew in all ends on wrong side.

Pie Crust

Crochet edging is worked into first row of loops where ribbing and purple body of hat meet.

Using 3 mm crochet hook, insert hook into purple purl loop. Sl st into next st. Work *3ch, dc into next purl loop, repeat from * right around hat. Finish off and sew in ends.

Blackberry Pie

Using 2.25 mm knitting needles and two strands of oatmeal, cast on 24 sts. Break off one strand of yarn and work 2 rows st st.

Row 3: *K1, k2tog, rep from * to end.

Row 4: Purl.

Row 5: K2tog, rep to end.

Break off yarn. Thread through rem sts, pull up tightly and fasten off.

To Make Up Sew the row ends together to make the base of the pie.

Filling

Using 2.25 mm knitting needles and purple 4-ply wool, cast on 16 sts.

Row 1: Purl.

Row 2: *K1, inc in next st, rep from * to end (24 sts).

Work 3 rows st st, beg with a purl row.

Row 6: * K1, k2tog, rep from * to end.

Row 7: P2tog, rep to end.

Break off yarn. Thread through rem sts, pull up tightly and fasten off.

Blackberries

Make one back and one front. Thread all the beads onto the purple 4-ply yarn.

Using 2 mm double-pointed needles and purple 4 ply cast on 3 sts.

Row 1: (wrong side) Inc in 1st st, p1, inc in last st (5 sts).

Row 2: (K1, mb) twice, k1.

Row 3: Inc in 1st st, p3, inc in last st (7 sts).

Rows 4, 6 and 8: (K1, mb) to last st, k1.

Row 5: Inc in 1st st, p5, inc in last st (9 sts).

Row 7: Inc in 1st st, p7, inc in last st (11sts).

Rows 9, 11, 13, 15 and 17: K1, p9, k1.

Rows 10 and 14: K2, (mb, k1) to last st, k1.

Rows 12 and 16: (K1, mb) to last st, k1.

Row 18: Sl1, k1, psso, (mb, k1) to last 3 sts, mb, k2tog (9 sts).

Row 19: K1, p7, k1.

Cast off.

Make 3.

Calyx

Using 2 mm double-pointed needles and green 4-ply cast on 8 sts.

Row 1: (wrong side) Cast off 5 sts, k2 (3 sts).

Row 2: K3, turn, cast on 5 sts (8 sts).

Repeat rows 1 and 2 four times.

Cast off.

To Make Up With right sides together sew blackberry, leaving top open. Turn right side out. Stuff quite firmly with fibre filling. Roll the calyx and secure along the cast off edge. Sew to the top of the blackberry. Pull into shape.

Leaves

Using 2.75 mm double-pointed needles and bright green 8-ply cast on 8 sts.

Row 1: Cast off 7 sts, leaving 1 st.

Inc row: (right side); K1, inc in st.

Row 2: Purl.

Row 3: K1, m1, k1, m1, k1.

Row 4 and all even rows: K first and last st and purl rem sts.

Row 5: K2, m1, k1, m1, k2.

Row 7: K3, m1, k1, m1, k3.

Row 9: K4, m1, k1, m1, k4.

Row 11: K5, m1, k1, m1, k5.

Rows 13 and 15: Knit.

Row 17: K5, sl2, k1, psso, k5.

Row 19: K4, sl2, k1, psso, k4.

Row 21: K3, sl2, k1, psso, k3.

Row 23: K2, sl2, k1, psso, k2.

Rows 24 and 26: Purl.

Row 25: K1, sl2, k1, psso, k1 (3 sts).

Row 27: K1, sl2, psso, fasten off.

Make 12

Press leaves to flatten into shape.

To Make Up

Sew row ends together and with the st st side facing out place filling over base. Fill with a little polyester fibre filling and stitch down around the inside of the base so your pie is plump.

Sew three leaves radiating out from the crown centre. Attach the pie to the top centre of the crown surrounded by the three blackberries. Arrange the rest of the leaves evenly between the top row of bobbles.

Autumn Harvest

With its toning colourways and autumnal motifs this fabulous headpiece is perfect for cooler days. Take your time when making the leaves and acorns, then set them aside to stitch onto the finished hat. If you prefer a simpler style knit just one or two different types of leaf. This is ideal for using up all those oddments of wool.

Size
To fit 18 months to 2 years

Materials
1 x 50 g ball olive green DK (8 ply)
1 x 50 g ball sage green DK (8 ply)
1 x 50 g ball chocolate brown DK (8 ply)
1 x 50 g ball beige DK (8 ply)
1 x 50 g ball lime green DK (8 ply)
1 x 50 g ball rust DK (8 ply)
2.75 mm double-pointed knitting needles
3.75 mm double-pointed knitting needles
3.5 mm crochet hook
Wool needle
Polyester fibre filling

Abbreviation

Mb (Make bobble): k1, p1, k1, p1, k1 into same st, turn, purl, turn, knit, turn, purl, turn, sl1, k1 **psso, k1, rep from ** until 1 st rem).

Using 3.75 mm double-pointed circular knitting needles and olive green cast on 90 sts. Mark the start point with a loop of another colour wool.

Work 10 rounds st st for rolled brim.

Fasten off the wool. Change to chocolate and rust and work in k1, p1 rib beginning with a knit st and alternating the colours with each stitch. Knit 11 rounds.

Next round: Knit using chocolate brown.

Next round: Purl using chocolate brown.

Next round: Knit using sage green.

Next round: Purl using sage green.

Chequerboard Pattern

Round 1: *K2 olive, k2 sage green, rep from * to end.

Round 2: As round 1.

Round 3: *K2 sage green, k2 olive green, rep from * to end of round.

Round 4: As round 3.

Rounds 5 and 6: As rounds 1 and 2.

Round 7: Knit using sage green.

Round 8: Purl using sage green.

Round 9: Knit using chocolate brown.

Round 10: Purl using chocolate brown.

Round 11: Join in rust and work 2 rounds st st.

Bobble round: Bobbles are worked in alternating colours of chocolate brown and beige. *K2 rust, make 1 bobble. Rep from * to end of round.

Rounds 13-15: Work using rust.

Round 16: Knit using chocolate brown.

Round 17: Purl using chocolate brown.

Rounds 18 and 19: Work using chocolate brown.

Rounds 20 and 21: Work using rust.

Rounds 22 and 23: Work using beige.

Round 24: Knit using chocolate brown.

Round 25: Purl using chocolate brown.

Crown Shaping

Working in beige:

Round 1: *K7, k2tog, rep from * to end.

Round 2 and all even rounds: Knit.

Round 3: *K6, k2tog, rep from * to end.

Round 5: *K5, k2tog, rep from * to end.

Continue pattern of decreasing until the round k1, k2tog has been worked. Break off yarn. Thread through rem sts, pull up tight and fasten off.

Acorn

Using 2.75 mm double-pointed circular knitting needles and chocolate brown, cast on 6 sts.

Row 1: (right side) Inc in each st (12 sts).

Row 2: Inc in each st (24 sts).

Row 3: *K1, p1, rep from * to end.

Row 4: *P1, k1, rep from * to end.

Rep rows 3 and 4 twice more.

Row 9: *P1, p2tog, rep from * to end.

Break off chocolate brown and join in beige. Commencing with a purl row, work 7 rows in st st.

Row 17: *K2tog, k2, rep from * to end.

Row 18: Purl.

Row 19: *K2tog, k1, rep from * to end.

Row 20: P2 4 times. Break off yarn, thread through rem 4 sts, pull up tightly and fasten off.
To make the stem, using chocolate brown, cast on 10 sts, cast off.

To Make Up Attach the stem to the cast on edge of the acorn. Join the seam with ladder stitch on the right side and fill firmly with polyester fibre filling as you sew the seam. Make 2.

Beech Leaf

Using 2.75 mm double-pointed circular knitting needles and olive, cast on 2 sts and make an I-Cord of 1.5 cm for the stem.

Inc row: K1, inc in this st, k1 (3 sts).

Row 2: Purl.

Row 3: K1 (Yo, k1) twice (5 sts).

Row 4: P1 (k1, p1) twice.

Row 5: K1, p1, yo, k1, yo, p1, k1 (7 sts.)

Row 6: P1, k1, p3, k1, p1.

Row 7: K1, p1, k1, yo, k1, yo, k1, p1, k1 (9 sts).

Row 8: P1 (k1, p1) 4 times.

Row 9: (K1, p1) twice, yo, k1, yo, (p1, k1 twice) 11 sts.

Row 10: (P1, k1) twice, p3, (k1, p1) twice.

Row 11: (K1, p1) twice, k1, yo, k1, yo, k1 (p1, k1) twice (13 sts).

Row 12: P1, (k1, p1) 6 times

Rows 13 and 14: Rib.

Row 15: Sl1, k1, psso, rib 9, k2tog (11 sts).

Row 16: Rib.

Row 17: Sl 1, k1, psso, rib 7, k2tog (9sts).

Row 18: Rib.

Row 19: Sl1, k1, psso, rib 5, K2tog (7sts).

Row 20: Rib.

Row 21: Sl1, k1, psso, rib 3, k2tog (5sts).

Row 22: Rib.

Row 23: Sl1, k1, psso, rib 1, k2tog (3sts).

Row 24: Rib.

Row 25: Sl2, k1 psso. Fasten off.

Whitebeam Leaf

Using 2.75 mm double-pointed circular knitting needles and olive, cast on 2 sts and make an I-Cord of 1.5 cm.

Inc row: K1, inc in this st, k1 (3 sts).

Row 2: Purl.

Row 3: K1, m1, k1, m1, k1 (5 sts).

Row 4 and all even rows: Knit first and last st, purl all others.

Row 5: K2, m1, k1, m1, k2 (7 sts).

Row 7: K3, m1, k1, m1, k3 (9 sts).

Row 9: K4, m1, k1, m1, k4 (11 sts).

Row 11: K5, m1, k1, m1, k5 (13 sts).

Row 13: K5, sl2, k1, psso, k5 (11 sts).

Row 15: K4, sl2, k1, psso, k4 (9 sts).
Row 17: K3 ,sl2, k1, psso, k3
(7 sts).
Row 19: K2, sl2, k1, psso, k2 (5 sts).
Row 21: K1, sl2, k1, psso, k1 (3 sts).
Row 23: Sl2, k1, psso, fasten off.
Make 2 more with lime green yarn.

Poplar Leaf

Using 2.75 mm double-pointed
circular knitting needles and
olive green cast on 10 sts. Cast
off 9 sts knitwise. Do not turn
work, leaving one st on right-hand
needle.
Row 1: K1, p1, k1 into same st (3 sts).
Turn.
Row 2: K1, p1, k1.
Row 3: K1, m1, sl1, m1, k1 (5 sts).
Row 4 and all even rows: Knit to
centre st, purl, knit to end.
Row 5: K2, m1, sl1, m1, k2 (7 sts).
Row 7: K3, m1, sl1, m1, k3 (9 sts).
Row 9: K4, m1, sl1, m1, k4 (11 sts).
Row 11: K5, m1, sl1, m1, k5 (13 sts).
Rows 13 and 15: Knit.
Row 17: K5, sl2, k1, psso, k5 (11 sts).
Row 19: K4, sl2, k1, psso, k4 (9 sts).
Row 21: K3, sl2, k1, psso, k3 (7 sts).
Row 23: K2, sl2, k1, psso, k2 (5 sts).
Row 25: K1, sl2, k1, psso, K1 (3 sts).
Row 27: Sl2, k1, psso, fasten off.

Maple Leaf

Using 2.75 mm double-pointed
circular knitting needles and
rust cast on 11 sts.
Row 1: (right side) K2, yo, k3, sl1, k3,
yo, k2 (13 sts).
**Row 2 and all even rows unless
stated otherwise**: Knit to centre
st, purl, knit to end.
Row 3: K2, yo, k4, sl1, k4, yo, k2
(15 sts).
Row 5: K2, yo, k5, sl1, k5, yo, k2
(17 sts).
Row 7: K2, yo, k6, sl1, k6, yo, k2
(19 sts).
Row 9: K2, yo, k7, sl1, k7, yo, k2
(21 sts).
Row 11: K2, yo, k8, sl1, k8, yo, k2
(23 sts).
Row 13: Cast off 6 sts, k5, sl1, k11
(17 sts).
Row 14: Cast off 6 sts, k5, p1, k5
(11 sts).
Row 15: As row 1.
Row 17: As row 3.
Row 19: As row 5.
Row 21: As row 7.
Row 23: Cast off 4 sts, k5, sl1, k9
(15 sts).
Row 24: Cast off 4 sts, k5, p1, k5
(11 sts).
Row 25: K3, sl1, k1, psso, sl1,
k2tog, k3 (9 sts).
Rows 26, 28, 30, 32: As row 2.
Row 27: K2, sl1, k1, psso, sl1, k2tog,
k2 (7 sts).
Row 29: K1, sl1, k1, psso, sl1, k2tog,
k1 (5sts).
Row 31: Sl1, k1, psso, sl1, k2tog
(3 sts).

Row 33: Sl2, k1, psso. Fasten off.
To make the stalk, using 2.75 mm
double-pointed needles and rust,
cast on 2 sts and make an I-Cord
of 3 cm. Fasten off. Attach to base
of leaf.
Make 2 more leaves using olive.
green

To Make Up

Sew in all ends. Arrange acorns
on top of hat and stitch in place.
Arrange the leaves around the top
of the crown in a pattern you like.
Stitch firmly in place.

Ho, Ho, Ho

Perfect for a stocking filler, this bright and colourful Christmas hat sets the tone perfectly with its cream holly leaves and red berries emanating from a central bobble on the crown. A soft mohair brim and snuggly wool make this hat are sure to make this a hit in the park.

Sizes
To fit 12-18 months (2-3) years

Materials
1 x 50 g ball cream mohair DK (8 ply)
1 x 50 g ball red DK (8 ply)
Small amount mid green DK (8 ply)
4 mm double-pointed knitting needles
2 x 2.25 mm double-pointed knitting needles
3 mm crochet hook
Wool needle
Polyester fibre filling

Abbreviation

Wrap: Bring yarn to front, slip next st from left to right needle, take yarn to back of work, return st to left-hand needle. This prevents holes in the work when turning.

Using 4 mm double-pointed knitting needles and cream mohair, cast on 92, (102) sts (30, 32, 30 / 33, 36, 33). Join into a ring being careful not to twist stitches.
Knit 10 rounds st st (every round knit).
Break off mohair and join in red. Work in k2, p2 rib for 12 (14) rounds.
Cont in st st for rem of hat, dec 2 (2) sts on first round.
Cont without further shaping until hat measures 15 (17) cm from rolled brim.

Crown Shaping

Next round: *K7 (8), k2tog, rep from * to end of round.
Next round: Knit (mid green).
Next round: *K6 (7), k2tog, rep from * to end of round.
Next round: Knit.
Next round: *K5 (6), k2tog, rep from * to end of round.
Continue decreasing in this manner until the round k2tog all round has been worked.
Break off yarn, thread through rem sts, pull up tightly and fasten off. Sew in all ends carefully on wrong side.

Bobble

Using 2.25 mm knitting needles and cream mohair, cast on 12 sts.
Row 1: Knit.
Row 2: P10, wrap.
Row 3: K8 , wrap.
Row 4: P6, wrap.
Row 5: K4, wrap.
Row 6: Purl.
Rep these 6 rows another 4 times. Cast off.
With right sides together, sew side seam half way. Turn right side out and stuff firmly. Sew the rest of the seam and then run a gathering thread around the cast-on edge. Pull up firmly and fasten off. Do the same with the other end. Stuff firmly with polyester fibre filling. Stitch firmly to top of crown

Holly Leaves

Round 1: (right side) Using 3 mm crochet hook and cream mohair make 12ch, miss 1ch,* 1dc in next ch, 1htr in next ch, 1tr in next ch, 2tr in next ch, 2dtr in next ch, 1dtr in next ch, 2dtr in next ch, 2tr in next ch, 1tr in next ch, 1htr in next ch, 1dc in next ch** 4ch, miss 1ch, ss in next ch, 1dc in next ch, working in remaining strand of 11 original base ch, repeat from *-** do not break yarn.
Stem: 9ch, miss 1ch, ss into each of the next 7ch, continue along sts of first round,*** 1dc in dc, 1dc in htr, 3ch, miss 1ch, ss in next ch, 1dc in next ch, 1dc in each of next 3 sts, (4ch, miss 1ch, ss in next ch, 1dc in next ch, 1htr in next ch, miss next st, 1dc in each of the next 3 sts) twice, 3 ch, miss 1ch, ss in next ch, 1dc in next ch, 1dc in next ch, 1dc in htr, ss in tr**** fasten off.
Second edge: Turn to ws to work along remaining straight edge of first round. Join mohair to 1ch above stem then work from ***-****. Fasten off.
Make at least four.

Holly Berries

Using 2.25 mm double-pointed knitting needles and red, cast on 1 st, k1, p1, k1, p1, k1 into same st (5 sts).
Row 1: Knit.
Row 2: Purl.
Row 3: Knit, do not turn, *sl second st over first, rep from * until 1 st rem, fasten off.

To Make Up Run a gathering thread around the outside of the bobble. Gather up tightly to form a round bobble. Attach 2 to the top of each holly leaf.

To Make Up

Sew the end of the holly stems to the top of the crown. Sew the pom pom on top.

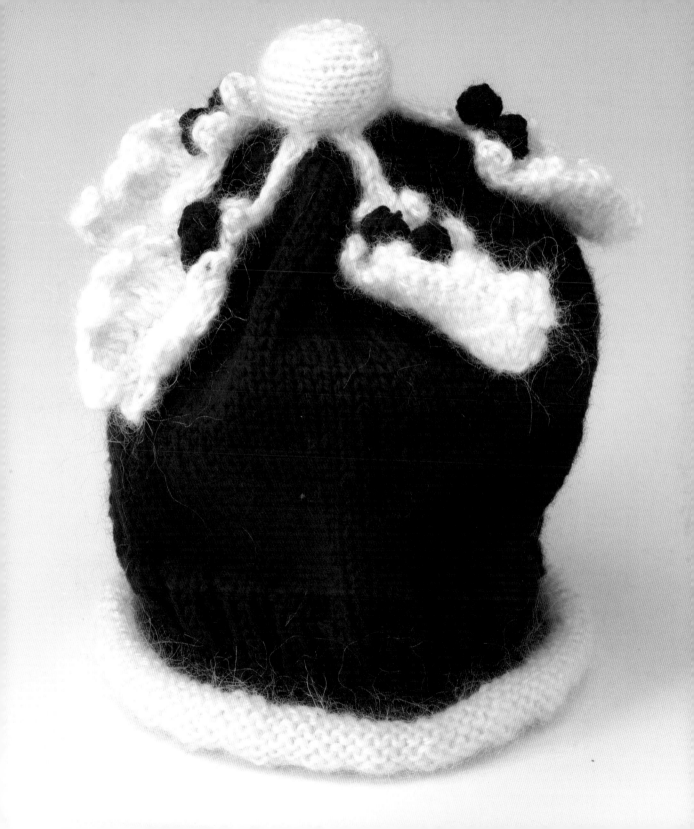

Fin's Penguin

My young grandson Fin loves all things penguin and in his short life I have made many penguin items. The body and head of this penguin are knitted in the round so he has a beautiful shape. His wings, feet and scarf are knitted on two needles. Some patience is required as the pieces are small, but the result is worthwhile.

Size
To fit 18 months to 2 years

Materials
1 x 50 g ball cream mohair DK (8 ply)

1 x 50 g ball red DK (8 ply)

1 x 50 g ball dark grey DK (8 ply)

Small amounts of 4 ply in red, black, white and orange

4 mm double-pointed knitting needles

2.25 mm double-pointed knitting needles

Polyester fibre filling

Wool needle

Abbreviation

Mb (make bobble): K1, p1, k1, p1, k1 into same st, turn, purl, turn, knit, turn, purl, turn, k1, sl1, k1, *psso, k1, rep from * until 1 st rem.

Using 4 mm double-pointed knitting needles and cream mohair, cast on 95 sts (32, 31, 32).
Knit one round.
Round 2: K2, *mb, k5, rep from * to last 2 sts, k3.
Round 3: Knit, dec 3 sts evenly (92 sts).
Break off cream and join in red and dark grey 8 ply.
Round 4-15: Work in k2 red, p2 dark grey rib for 12 rounds.
Rounds 16-18: Using dark grey 8 ply, knit 1 round, purl 1 round, knit 1 round.
Round 19: Knit using cream

mohair.
Round 20: K2, *mb, k4, rep from * to last 2 sts, k2.
Rounds 21 and 22: Knit.
Rounds 23-25: Join in dark grey 8 ply, knit 1 round, purl 1 round, knit 1 round.
Round 26: Knit using cream mohair.
Round 27: K4, *mb, k4, rep from * end.
Rounds 28-29: Knit.
Rounds 30-32 Swap to dark grey, knit 1 round, purl 1 round, knit 1 round.
Round 33: Knit using cream mohair.
Round 34: K2, *mb, k4, rep from * to last 2 sts, k2.
Rounds 35 and 36: Knit using cream mohair..
Rounds 37-39: Swap to dark grey,

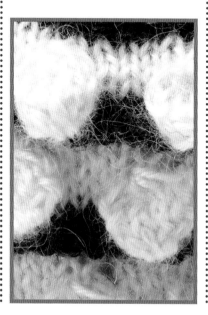

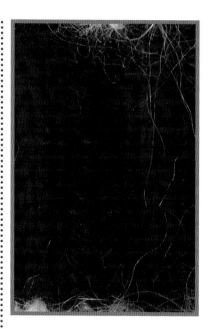

knit 1 round, purl 1 round, knit 1 round.
Round 40: Knit using cream mohair.
Round 41: K4, *mb, k4, rep from * to end.
Rounds 42-43: Knit using cream mohair.

Crown Shaping
Work in alternate rows of red and dark grey.
Round 1: * K7, k2tog, rep from * to end of round.
Round 2: Knit.
Round 3: *K6, k2tog, rep from * to end of round.
Round 4: Knit.
Round 5: *K5, k2tog, rep from * to end of round.
Continue decreasing in this

manner until the round k2tog all round has been worked.

Break off yarn, thread through rem sts, pull up tightly and fasten off. Sew in all ends carefully on wrong side.

Penguin

Head

Using 2.25 mm double-pointed knitting needles and black 4 ply, cast on 9 sts (3, 3, 3). Join into a ring being careful not to twist the sts.

Round 1: Knit.

Round 2: *K1, m1, k1, m1, k1, rep from * to end of round (15 sts). ** Work 4 rounds st st without further shaping.

Round 7: * Sl1, psso, k1, k2tog, rep from * to end of round (9 sts).

Round 8: Knit.

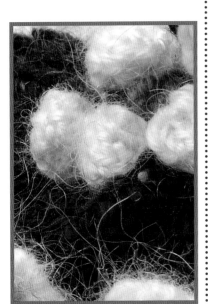

Round 9: Carefully and firmly fill head with polyester fibre filling. Break off yarn, thread through rem sts, pull up tightly and fasten off.

Body

Work as for head using black 4-ply until **.

Round 3: Knit.

Round 4: *K1, m1, k3, m1, k1, rep from *to end of round.

Work a further 7 rounds st st without shaping.

Round 12: * Sl1, k1, psso, k3, k2tog, rep from * to end of round.

Round 13: Knit.

Round 14: *Sl1, psso, k1, k2tog, rep from * to end of round (9 sts).

Round 15: Knit.

Firmly stuff body with polyester fibre filling. Break off yarn, thread through rem sts, pull

up tightly and fasten off.

Tummy

Using 2 x 2.25 mm double-pointed needles and white 4 ply, cast on 3 sts.

Row 1: Purl.

Row 2: Inc in first and last st (5 sts).

Begin with a purl row work 17 rows st st.

Row 20: Sl1, k1 , psso, k1, k2tog.

Row 21: Purl.

Row 22: Sl1, k2tog, psso.

Fasten off.

Centre the tummy panel lengthways on the front body and sew in place with very small stitches.

Face

Using 2 x 2.25 mm double-pointed needles and white 4 ply, cast on 1 st.

Knit 1 row.

Row 2: Inc in front and back of st (3 sts).

Row 3: Purl.

Row 4: Inc in first and last st (5 sts).

Row 5: Purl. Cast off.

Stitch with the point facing down to the head. Attach the head firmly to the top of the body. Align the face with the top of the tummy piece.

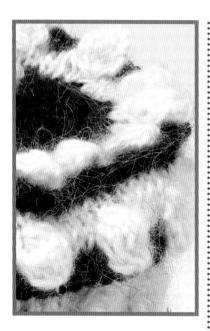

Wings

Using 2 x 2.25 mm double-pointed needles and black 4 ply, cast on 3 sts.

Row 1: Purl.

Row 2: Inc in first and last st (5 sts).

Begin with a purl row, work 11 rows st st.

Row 14: Sl1, k1, psso, k1, k2tog.

Row 15: Purl.

Row 16: Sl1, k2tog, psso.

Fasten off.

Attach a wing to the neckline at each side of the body using the cast on edge.

Beak

Using 2 x 2.25 mm double-pointed needles and orange 4 ply, cast on 3 sts.

Work 3 rows garter st. Cast off. Roll up very tightly into a tube and stitch closed. Attach to the centre of the face.

Eyes

Make 2 eyes with 3 strands of black embroidery thread. Work a bullion knot for each eye. Tie off under the neckline.

Feet

Using 2 x 2.25 mm double-pointed needles and orange 4 ply, cast on 9 sts. Work in k1, p1 rib throughout.

Row 1: Dec 1 st at each end of row. Keeping rib pattern correct, rep this row until 3 sts remain.

Work 1 row rib.

Next row: Inc 1 st at each end of row.

Keeping rib pattern correct repeat this row until there are 9 sts.

Cast off in rib.

To Make Up Fold piece in half and stitch around the row ends. Attach to the underside of the penguin with the widest end facing forwards.

Scarf

Using 2 x 2.25 mm double-pointed needles and red 4 ply, cast on 3 sts. Work in garter st (every row knit), until scarf measures 10 cm. Cast off. Tie in a knot around penguin's neck.

Snowballs

Using 2 x 2.25 mm double-pointed needles and cream mohair 4 ply, cast on 1 st. Work a bobble. When 1 stitch remains. Break off yarn and fasten off. Make as many as you like.

To Make Up

Attach penguin to crown of hat. Sew snowballs around the penguin. Do not press or you will flatten the bobbles.

Frog in a Pond

Any frog fan will be delighted with this tiny creature sitting atop his leaves in the centre of the pond. This hat provides a challenge for the advancing knitter. Take the time to make your frog carefully as it will be the focus of attention.

Size
To fit 18 months to 2 years

Materials
1 x 50 g ball lime green DK (8 ply)

1 x 50 g ball sage green DK (8 ply)

1 x 50 g ball light blue DK (8 ply)

1 x 50 g ball bright blue DK (8 ply)

1 x 50 g ball Baby, Dolce Amore by Filatura Di Crosa, shade 48

Small amount green 4-ply cotton

Black stranded embroidery cotton

2.25 mm double-pointed knitting needles

Polyester fibre filling

3.75 mm double-pointed knitting needles

Wool needle

3.5 mm crochet hook

Abbreviation

Mb (make bobble): k1, p1, k1, p1, k1 into same st, turn, purl, turn, knit, turn, purl, turn, knit, sl1, k1, *psso, k1, rep from * until 1 st rems.

Tension

24 sts to 10 cm worked on 3.75 mm needles, worked over st st.

Using 3.75 mm double-pointed knitting needles and lime green, cast on 92 sts on 3 needles (30, 32, 30).
Work 10 rounds st st (knit every round).
Round 11: Join in light blue and work k2 light blue, p2 lime green rib for 13 rounds.
Round 24: Knit using lime green, decreasing 2 sts on this round on 2nd needle (90 sts).

Round 25: Purl using lime green.
Round 26: Knit using sage green.
Round 27: Purl using sage green.
Round 28: Knit using light blue.
Round 29: Purl using light blue.
Round 30: Knit using bright blue.
Round 31: Purl using bright blue.
Knit 2 rounds light blue.
Bobble round: Using light blue *k4, mb, rep from * to end.
Work another 2 rounds light blue.
Round 37: Knit using bright blue.
Round 38: Purl using bright blue.
Next 8 rounds: Place graph repeating it nine times over six rows.
Round 47: Knit using bright blue.
Round 48: Purl using bright blue.
Round 49: Knit using bright blue.
Round 50: Purl using light blue.
Round 51: Knit using sage green.
Round 52: Purl using sage green.
Round 53: Knit using lime green.

Round 54: Purl using lime green.

Crown Shaping

Round 1: Using blue for remainder *k7, k2tog, rep from * to end.
Round 2 and all even rounds: Knit.
Round 3: *K6, k2tog, rep from * to end.
Round 5: *K5, k2tog, rep from * to end.
Continue decreasing in this manner until the round k1, k2tog has been worked. Break off yarn. Thread through rem sts, pull up tight and fasten off.

Sew in all ends.

Frog

Using 2.25 mm double-pointed knitting needles and Dolce Amore cast on 3 sts on each needle. Form in to a circle, being careful not to twist the ring (9 sts).

Round 1: Knit.

Round 2: *K1, m1, rep from * to end of round (15 sts).

Work 4 rounds st st without shaping.

Round 7: *Sl, k1, psso, k1, k2tog, rep from * to end (9 sts).

Round 8: Knit.

Leave sts on needle, stuff head firmly to make a round shape, then thread yarn through rem sts, pull up tightly and fasten off.

Eyes, Feet and Hands

These are all made as a bobble and then sewn on to the head or ends of arms or legs. Make 6.

Using 2.25 mm double-pointed knitting needles and Dolce Amore cast on 1 st.

Row 1: Knit into the front, back and front again (3 sts).

Row 2: Knit.

Row 3: Purl.

Row 4: Knit, don't turn work, pass 2nd, 3rd and 4th sts one at a time over the first st. Fasten off. Work running stitch around the outside and pull up to form a bobble.

Body

Using 2.25 mm double-pointed knitting needles and Dolce Amore cast on 3 sts on each needle. Form in to a circle, being careful not to twist the ring (9 sts).

Round 1: Knit.

Round 2: *K1, m1, rep from * to end of round (15 sts).

Work 4 rounds st st without shaping.

Round 7: Knit.

Round 8: *K1, m1, k3, m1, k1, rep from * to end (21 sts).

Work 4 rounds st st without shaping.

Round 13: *Sl1, k1, psso, k3, k2tog, rep from * to end (15 sts).

Round 14: Knit.

Round 15: *Sl1, k1, psso, k1, k2tog, rep from * to end (9sts).

Round 16: Knit.

Leave sts on needle, stuff body firmly to make a round shape. Then thread yarn through rem sts, pull up tightly and fasten off.

Legs and Arms

Using 2.25 mm double-pointed knitting needles and Dolce Amore cast on 2 sts make an I-Cord of 3 cm. Knit one row, do not turn, *slide sts to other end of needle and pull yarn firmly behind, knit next row. Repeat from * until cord is desired length. Sl1, k2tog, psso, fasten off. Make 4.

To Make Up Sew head firmly to body. Stitch arms to shoulders. Position legs at each side of body and stitch into place. Sew a bobble hand or foot bobble onto the end of each arm and leg.

Stitch the eyes to the top of the head using the photograph as a guide. Work a French knot in black embroidery cotton in the centre of each eye and give your frog a lovely big smile by taking a wide stitch across the centre of his face and anchoring with a tiny stitch in the centre. Fasten off under the body of the frog.

Leaves

Make 6 in sage green and 7 in lime green. Using 3.5 mm crochet hook and green 4 ply, make 10ch. Slip last st on to 3.75 mm double-

pointed knitting needles and work as follows:

Row 1: (right side) K1, inc, k1.

Row 2: Purl.

Row 3: K1, m1, k1, m1, k1.

Row 4 and all even rows: Knit first and last st and purl rem sts.

Row 5: K2, m1, k1, m1, k2.

Row 7: K3 m1, k1, m1, k3.

Row 9: K4, m1, k1, m1, k4.

Row 11: K5, m1, k1, m1, k5.

Rows 13 and 15: Knit.

Row 17: K5, sl2, k1, psso, k5.

Row 19: K4, sl2, k1, psso, k4.

Row 21: K3, sl2, k1, psso, k3.

Row 23: K2, sl2, k1, psso, k2.

Rows 24 and 26: Purl.

Row 25: K1, sl2, k1, psso, k1 (3 sts).

Row 27: K1, sl2, psso, fasten off.

Attach 12 leaves in a circle to the top of the hat. Stitch the frog to the centre of the remaining leaf and then stitch this leaf to the

centre of the crown.

Hop To It

Fans of rabbits will be delighted with this beanie, which features a frieze of carrots and a plump white bunny clutching a juicy carrot in his tiny white paw. Variegated leaves decorate the crown. Take your time finishing this off and you will end up with a fantastic result.

Sizes
To fit 18 months to 2 years (3-4 years)

Materials

1 x 50 g ball bright green DK (8 ply)
Small amounts of olive green, mid green, mid brown, and orange DK (8 ply)
Small amounts of white and orange cotton 4 ply
Stranded embroidery cotton in black and pink
Polyester fibre filling

4 mm double-pointed knitting needles
2.25 mm double-pointed knitting needles
2.75 mm double-pointed knitting needles
Wool needle
Embroidery needle

Using 4 mm double-pointed knitting needles and mid brown DK (8 ply) cast on 90 (100) sts on 3 needles. Join into a ring being careful not to twist the stitches. Work 10 rounds in st st. Break off mid brown and join in bright green. Work 12 (14) rounds k1, p1 rib. Work 2 rounds of st st.

Work 14 rounds of carrot pattern as follows:

Round 1: K2 green, *k1 orange, k9 green, rep from * ending with k7 green.

Round 2: As round 1.

Round 3: K2 green, *k2 orange, k8 green, rep from * ending with k6 green.

Round 4: As round 3.

Round 5: K2 green, *k3 orange, k7 green, rep from * ending with k5 green.

Round 6: As round 5.

Round 7: K3 green, *k3 orange, k8 green, rep from * ending with k4 green.

Round 8: As round 7.

Round 9: K3 green, *k4 orange, k6 green, rep from * ending with k3 green.

Round 10: K4 green, *k3 green, k7 green, rep from * ending with k3 green.

Round 11: As round 10.

Round 12: K4 green, *k4 mid green, k6 green, rep from * ending with k2 green.

Round 13: K5 green, *k3 mid green, k7 green, rep from * ending with k2 green.

Round 14: Knit in green.
There will be 9 carrots for the smaller size and 10 carrots for the larger hat.

Round 15: Knit bright green. Break off bright green and join in mid brown.

Round 16: Knit.

Round 17: Purl.

Round 18: Knit.

Round 19: Purl.
Break off mid brown and join in orange.

Round 20: Knit.

Round 21: Purl.

Round 22: Knit.

Round 23: Purl.
Break off orange and join in bright green. Knit one round.

Crown Shaping

Work in alternating rounds of bright green and mid green.

Round 1: Bright green *K7 (8), k2tog, rep from * to end of round.

Round 2: Knit using mid green.

Round 3: *K6 (7), k2tog, rep from * to end of round.

Round 4: Knit.

Round 5: *K5 (6), k2tog, rep from * to end of round.
Continue decreasing in this manner until the round k2tog all round has been worked.
Break off yarn, thread through rem sts, pull up tightly and fasten off. Sew in all ends carefully on wrong side.

Rabbit

Head

Using 2.25 mm double-pointed knitting needles and white 4 ply, cast on 9 sts (3, 3, 3). Join into a ring.

Round 1: Knit.

Round 2: K1, m1, k1, on each needle (15 sts).

Round 3: Knit.

Round 4: K1, m1, k3, m1, k1 (21 sts).

Rounds 5-8: Knit.

Round 9: K1, k2tog, k1, k2tog, k1 (15 sts).

Rounds 10 and 11: Knit.

Round 12: Sl1, k1, psso, k1, k2tog (9 sts).

Round 13: Knit.

Leaving sts on needle, stuff head firmly. Run thread through rem sts, pull up tightly and fasten off. Set aside for later.

Body

Using 2.25 mm double-pointed needles and white cotton 4 ply cast on 9 sts (3, 3, 3). Join into a ring.

Round 1: Knit.

Round 2: K1, m1, k1, m1, k1 on each needle (15 sts).

Round 3: Knit.

Round 4: K1, m1, k3, m1, k1, (21 sts).

Round 5: Knit.

Round 6: K1, m1, k5, m1, k1 (27 sts).

Rounds 7-15: Knit.

Round 16: Sl1, k1, psso, k5, k2tog on each needle (21 sts).

Round 17: Knit.

Round 18: Sl1, k1, psso, k3, k2tog, on each needle (15 sts).

Round 19: Knit.

Round 20: Sl1, k1, psso, k1, k2tog, on each needle (9 sts).

Round 20: Knit.

Leaving sts on needle, stuff body firmly. Run thread through rem sts, pull up tightly and fasten off. Set aside.

Ears

Using 2.25 mm double-pointed needles and white cotton 4 ply and working backwards and forwards in rows, cast on 2 sts.

Row 1 and odd rows: Purl.

Row 2: K1, m1, k1.

Row 4: K1, m1, k1, m1, k1.

Work 15 rows st st ending with a purl row.

Row 20: K2tog, k1, k2tog.

Row 21: Purl.

Cast off. Make 2.

I-Cord Legs and Arms

Using 2.25 mm double-pointed needles and white cotton 4 ply cast on 3 sts.

Row 1: *Knit. Do not turn, slide sts to the other end of the needle, pull yarn firmly behind the work and repeat the first row. Continue in this manner until your I-Cord is the desired length then sl1, k2tog, psso, fasten off.

Make two I-Cords 3.5 cm long for the arms. Make two I-Cords 5 cm long for the legs.

Feet, Paws and Tail

These are made like a bobble and then stitched to the end of the leg or the arm. Make 5 in total.

Using 2.25 mm double-pointed needles and white cotton 4 ply cast on 1 st.

K1, p1, k1, p1, k1 into this stitch (5 sts). Turn, purl. Turn, knit. Turn,purl. Turn, knit. Do not turn. Slip the second stitch over the first on the right-hand needle. Cont in this manner until 1st rems. Break off yarn. Thread through st. Pull up tightly and fasten off. To form into a bobble. Run a gathering stitch around the outside edge, draw up and fasten off. Attach one to each arm and leg and keep one for the tail.

Scarf

Using 2.25 mm double-pointed needles and orange cotton 4 ply and working backwards and forwards in rows, cast on 3 sts. Work in k1, p1 rib for 11 cm. Cast off. Sew in ends.

Carrot

Using 2.25 mm double-pointed needles and orange cotton 4 ply and working backwards and forwards in rows, cast on 1 st. Work in garter st.
Knit 1 row.
Row 2: Inc (2 sts).
Row 3: Knit.
Row 4: K1, inc (3 sts).
Cont increasing 1 st in the centre of the row until there are 6 sts.
Work 1 row.
Cast off.
Cut a couple of short pieces of green yarn for the carrot tops. Roll up the carrot. Stitch up the side seam enclosing the carrot tops in place as you go.
To Make Up Using 3 strands of black embroidery cotton, make French knots for eyes on each side

of head. Use pink to embroider the nose. Secure the threads where the head will attach to the body. Pin the ears on the back of the head and sew firmly in place. Sew the head to the body ensuring it is evenly placed and then sew the arms to each side of the body. Sew the carrot firmly to one paw. Sew the legs to the body at the hips. Dress the rabbit with the scarf. Set aside.

Leaves

Make 9, 3 in olive green , 3 in bright green and 3 in mid green. Using 2.75 mm double-pointed knitting needles and bright green 8 ply, cast on 3 sts and make a 2 cm I-Cord following the instructions for the arms and legs. Continue to knit the leaf as follows:

Row 1: Knit.

Row 2: Purl.

Row 3: K1, m1, k1tbl, m1, k1.

Row 4 and all even rows: Knit first and last st, purl sts between.

Row 5: K2, m1, k1tbl, m1, k2.

Row 7: K3, m1, k1tbl, m1, k3.

Row 9: K4, m1, k1tbl, m1, k4.

Row 11: K5, m1, k1tbl, m1, k5.

Row 13: K5, sl2, k1, psso, k5.

Row 15: K4, sl2, k1, psso, k4.

Row 17: K3, sl2, k1, psso, k3.

Row 19: K2, sl2, k1, psso, k2.

Row 21: K1, sl2, k1, psso, k1.

Row 23: Sl2, k1, psso, fasten off.

Attach 6 leaves to the crown of the hat leaving a space in the centre for the rabbit. Press the hat if needed and then stitch the rabbit firmly in place. Sew in any loose ends. Stitch the remaining 2 leaves just under the brown and orange garter stitch border, to the right of the rabbit.

Plum in the Garden

I made this hat after an afternoon of gardening with my little cat Plum. There is nothing he loves more than poking around in the pots, often digging out the little seedlings I have planted and knocking over the containers. Make your playful kitten in the colour of your choice.

Size
To fit 18 months to 2 years

Materials
1 x 50 g ball mid brown DK (8 ply)
1 x 50 g ball terracotta DK (8 ply)
1 x 50 g ball olive green DK (8 ply)
1 x 50 g ball orange DK (8 ply)
Small amounts of DK (8 ply) in
    yellow, sage green and
    oatmeal
Small amounts of 4 ply in yellow,
    orange, cream, terracotta,
    jade and sapphire

Small amount Lacey Lamb grey
    2 ply or a combination of 3-ply
    baby wool and Rowan Kid Silk
    Haze
Small amount Rowan Kid Silk Haze
    dark grey
Polyester fibre filling
Cardboard scraps, cut to the size of
    a small coin
Wool needle

Stranded embroidery cotton in
    pink and green
Embroidery needle
4 mm double-pointed knitting
    needles, plus 1 spare
2 mm knitting kneedles, plus
    1 spare
2 x 2.75 mm double-pointed
    knitting kneedles
3 mm crochet hook

Abbreviations

Mb (make bobble) K1, p1, k1, p1, k1 into same stitch (5 sts), turn, purl, turn, knit, turn, purl, knit. Pass, second st, on right-hand needle over first st. Repeat until 1 st remains on right-hand needle.
Kt (knitted twirl): With contrast colour and spare double-pointed knitting needle knit into next st and cast on 12 sts. Turn. Cast off.

Using 4 mm double-pointed knitting needles and mid brown, 8 ply, cast on 90 sts (30, 30, 30). Join into a ring being careful not to twist sts.
Work 10 rows st st (every row knit).
Break off mid brown and join in terracotta 8 ply.
Knit 1 round terracotta.
Join in olive green 8 ply
Work in k1 terracotta, pl 1 olive

green rib for 14 rounds.
Round 16: Purl using terracotta.
Round 17: Knit using orange.
Round 18: Purl using orange.
Work 2 rounds st st using terracotta.
Bobble round: Using orange k2, *mb, k4 rep from * ending round with k2.
Work 2 rounds st st terracotta.
Round 24: Purl using orange.
Round 25: Knit using orange.
Round 26: Purl using terracotta.
Round 27: Knit using orange.
Knitted twirl round: There are 10 twirls knitted into this rounds 4 green, 3 yellow and 3 oatmeal. K4,*kt green, k8, rep from * ending round with k4. alternating colours (green, yellow and oatmeal. There will be one extra green to place).
Knit another 2 rounds orange.
Round 31: Purl using orange.

Round 32: Knit using orange.
Round 33: Purl using terracotta.
Break off orange and terracotta and join in mid brown.
Work 2 rounds st st mid brown.
Bobble round: Using oatmeal k2, *mb, k4 rep from * ending round with k2.
Work another 2 rounds st st mid brown.
Round 39: Purl using mid brown
Join in olive green.

Crown Shaping

Work in alternating stripes of one round mid brown and one round olive green.
Round 1: *K7, k2tog, rep from * to end of round.
Round 2: Knit.
Round 3: *K6, k2tog, rep from * to end of round.
Round 4: Knit.
Round 5: *K5, k2tog, rep from * to end of round.
Continue decreasing in this manner until the round k2tog all round has been worked.
Break off yarn, thread through rem sts, pull up tightly and fasten off.
Sew in all ends on wrong side.

Leaves

Make 4 from sage green and 4 from olive green DK (8 ply). Using 2.75 mm double-pointed knitting needles, cast on 3 sts.

Row 1: *Knit, do not turn work, pull sts to the other end of needle, pull yarn firmly behind. Rep from * until I-Cord is the right length. Work backwards and forwards in rows.

Row 2: K1, yfd, k1, yfd, k1.

Row 3 and all odd rows: Knit.

Row 4: K2, yfd, k1, yfd, k2.

Row 6: K3, yfd, k1, yfd, k3.

Row 8: K4, yfd, K1, yfd, k4.

Row 10: K5, yfd, K1, yfd, k5.

Row 12: Sl1, k1, psso, k9, k2tog.

Row 14: Sl1, k1, psso, k7, k2tog.

Row 16: Sl1, k1, psso, k5, k2tog.

Row 18: Sl1, k1, psso, k3, k2tog.

Row 20: Sl1, k1, psso, k1, k2tog.

Row 22: Sl2, k1, psso, Fasten off.

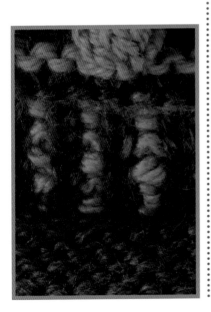

Flowers

Make 12. Use contrasting colours for petals and flower centre. Using 3 mm crochet hook and 4 ply make 4ch, join with a ss, into a ring.

Round 1: (right side) 2ch, 9dc in ring, ss to top of 2ch (10 sts).

Round 2: With contrasting 4 ply 5ch, 1 tr in each of next 9dc, ss to top of 5ch. Fasten off.

To Make Up Sew in ends and form into a neat circular shape. Turn the right way out.

Flowerpots

Using 2 mm knitting needles and terracotta 4 ply, cast on 30 sts using 2 strands of yarn.

Knit 1 row using 1 strand of yarn. Commencing with a knit row, work 8 rows of st st.

Row 10: *K3, k2tog, rep from * to end of row.

Commencing with a purl row, work 4 rows st st.

Row 15: Knit.

Row 16: *P2, p2tog, rep from * to end of row.

Row 17: Knit.

Row 18: *P1, p2tog, rep from * to end of row.

Row 19: K2tog to end.

Break off yarn, thread through rem sts, pull up tightly and fasten off. Make 3.

To Make Up With right sides together, stitch up seam. Sew in ends and insert cardboard coin into base of pot. Stuff firmly with polyester fibre filling to make a rounded shape. Sew three flowers to the top of each flowerpot, ensuring that the polyester fibre filling is covered. Catch the edges of the flowers to the edges of the flowerpot and sew the edges of the flowers to each other so that the flowerpots look plump and full. There will be 3 flowers left over.

Kitten
Head

Using 2 mm knitting needles and using 1 strand Lacey Lamb and 1 strand of Rowan Kid Silk Haze together, cast on 8 sts.

Row 1: Purl.

Row 2: Inc in every st (16 sts).

Row 3: Purl.

Row 4: K2, inc in next 2 sts, k11, inc 2 sts, k3 (24 sts).

Row 5: Purl.

Row 6: K3, inc in next 2 sts, k13, inc in next 2 sts, k4 (28 sts).

Work 3 rows st st, mark the centre of the first row.

Row 7: Purl.

Row 8: K4, k2tog (twice), k13, k2tog, (twice), k3 (24 sts).

Row 9: Purl.

Row 10: K3, k2tog (twice), k11, k2tog, (twice), k2 (20 sts).

Row 11: Purl.

Row 12: K2, k2tog (twice), k19, k2tog, (twice), k1 (16 sts).

Row 13: P2tog all across.

Break off yarn, thread through rem sts, pull up tightly and fasten off. Join row ends. leaving a gap for stuffing at the centre back of the head. Gather the cast on stitches. Stuff firmly. Shape head to make a firm round shape. Set aside.

Face

Using 3 strands of green embroidery cotton, work a couple of straight stitches for the eyes, and then a bullion knot on each side of the centre point.

Using 3 strands of pink embroidery cotton stitch a pink triangle for the nose and a few straight stitches for the mouth. The whiskers are formed from dark grey Kid Silk Haze. Be sure to knot firmly so they can't be easily pulled out. Knot the embroidery cotton under the neck where it will be hidden where the head attaches to the body.

Legs and Body

Using 2 mm knitting needles and 1 strand of Lacey Lamb grey and 1 strand of Rowan Kid Silk Haze grey together, cast on 6 sts.

Row 1 Inc into every st (12 sts). Commencing with a purl row, st st 11 rows.*

Break off yarn and leave these sts on a spare needle.

Work a second leg to match as far as *.

With right sides facing knit across both sets of stitches (24 sts). Commencing with a purl row, work another 15 rows.

Next row: *K2, k2tog, rep from * to end (18 sts).

Next row: Purl.

Next row: *K1, k2tog, rep from * to end 12sts.

Next row: Purl.

Next row: K2tog all across. Break off yarn, thread through rem sts, pull up tightly and fasten off.

To Make Up Take your time when stitching the kitten together. Because the pieces are small it is easier to sew him together with the right sides out. The reverse st st side is the right side out. Join row ends of paws with wrong sides together. Stuff paws firmly, then close tummy seam, leaving a gap for stuffing. Stuff very firmly to give a firm round shape. Attach head to top of paws, angling slightly to give a cheeky aspect.

Ears

Using 2 mm knitting needles and 1 strand of Lacey Lamb grey and 1 strand of Rowan Kid Silk Haze grey together, cast on 7 sts. Work 4 rows garter st, decreasing 1 st at each end of next and foll rows until 3 sts rem.

Next row: Sl2, k1, psso, Fasten off Make 2.

Pin the ears to each side of the head. Sew firmly into place, curving around the side of the head as you sew, to form a realistic shape.

Tail

Using 2 mm knitting needles and
1 strand of Lacey Lamb grey and
1 strand of Rowan Kid Silk Haze
grey together, cast on 2 sts.
Work in st st and inc 1 st at the beg
of every row until there are 8 sts.
Work another 6 rows st st.
Next row: Dec 1 st at the end of
the next row.
Work another 5 rows st st.
Next row: Dec 1 st at the end of
the next row.
Work another 5 rows.
Next row: K2tog to end.
Break off yarn, thread through rem
sts, pull up tightly and fasten off.
Fold tail in half, stitch closed carefully. Sew in place so that the tail
sits up jauntily.
Knot a length of yarn around the
kitten's neck for the collar.

Adding decorations

Sew in all ends neatly. Firmly sew
the kitten to the centre of the
crown. Arrange the three
flowerpots around the kitten.
Holding one in place stitch firmly
all around the base so that it
stands up. The other two lie on
their sides as if the kitten has
knocked them over. Stitch firmly to
the crown. Sew the three remaining flowers in front of the kitten.
Finally sew the eight leaves evenly
around the crown between the
oatmeal bobbles.

Rabbit in a Hat

Who could resist this dear little rabbit sitting among the flowers on top of a cosy beanie? If the hat is for a boy, you could omit the flowers. Make the rabbit and flowers first and set aside until the rest of the hat is complete.

Size
To fit 2–4 years

Materials

1 x 50 g ball white Baby Dolce Amore by Filatura Di Crosa or other 4 ply

1 x 50 g ball blue Baby Dolce Amore by Filatura Di Crosa or other 4 ply

1 x 50 g ball white DK (8 ply)

1 x 50 g ball aqua DK (8 ply)

1 x 50 g ball bright blue DK (8 ply)

1 x 50 g ball mid blue DK (8 ply)

Small amounts of 4 ply in bright blue, yellow, white and mid blue

3.75 mm double-pointed knitting needles

2.25 mm double-pointed knitting needles

3 mm crochet hook

Wool needle

Polyester fibre filling

Rabbit

Head

Using 2.25 mm double-pointed knitting needles and white 4 ply cotton, cast on 9 sts, 3 on each needle. Being careful not to twist the sts, join into a round.

Round 1: Knit.

Round 2: *K1, m1, rep from * to end of round (15 sts).

Round 3: Knit.

Round 4: K1, m1, k3, m1, k1 on each needle (21 sts).

Work 3 rounds st st.

Round 8: K1, k2tog, k1, k2tog, k1 on each needle (15 sts).

Work 2 rounds st st.

Round 11: Sl1, k1, psso, k1, k2tog on each needle (9 sts).

Round 12: Knit.

Stuff head firmly.

Round 12: K1, k2tog on each needle.

Break off yarn and thread through rem sts, pull up tightly and fasten off.

Run a gathering thread around opening at other end of head and close securely. Set head aside.

Ears

Using two 2.25 mm double-pointed knitting needles and white 4-ply cotton, cast on 3 sts.

Purl 1 row.

Next row: Inc in first and last st. Beg with a purl row work 13 rows st st.

Next row: Sl1, k1, psso, k1, k2tog.

Next row: Purl.

Next row: Sl1, k2tog, psso. Fasten off.

Make 2.

Body

The body is worked in alternating stripes of 2 rows white cotton and 2 rows blue.

Using 2.25 mm double-pointed knitting needles and white 4-ply cotton, cast on 9 sts, 3 on each needle. Join into a round, being careful not to twist the stitches.

Round 1: Knit.

Round 2: *K1, m1, rep from * to end of round (15 sts).

Round 3: Knit.

Round 4: K1, m1, k3, m1, k1 on each needle (21 sts).

Round 5: Knit.

Round 6: K1, m1, k5, m1, k1 on each needle (27 sts).

Rounds 7-13: Stocking stitch.

Round 14: Sl1, k1, psso, k5, k2tog on each needle (21 sts).

Round 15: Knit.

Round 16: Sl1, k1, psso, k3, k2tog on each needle (15 sts).

Round 17: Knit.

Round 18: Sl1, k1, psso, k1, k2tog on each needle (9 sts).

Stuff the body as for the head, taking care to fill firmly. Cut the yarn, thread through rem sts, pull up tightly and fasten off. Run a gathering thread around hole at other end and secure firmly.

Arms and Legs

Using 2.25 mm double-pointed knitting needles and white 4-ply cotton, cast on 2 sts and make an I-Cord 5 cm long. Fasten off by k2tog. Make 4.

Feet

Using 2.25 mm double-pointed knitting needles and blue 4-ply cotton, cast on 3 sts.
Purl 1 row.
Next row: Inc in first and last st.
Next row: Inc in first and last st.
Work 5 rows st st commencing with a purl row.
Next row: Knit (ridge).
Work another 5 rows st st.
Next row: Sl1, k1, psso, knit to last 2 sts, k2tog.
Next row: P2tog, purl to last 2 sts, p2tog tbl.
Cast off.
Make 2.
Fold the foot in half at the ridge line and stitch to the foot with the narrowest end pointing forwards. Fold the foot in half to make a narrow triangular shape and stitch in place along the underside.

Paws

Using 2.25 mm double-pointed knitting needles and blue 4-ply cotton, cast on 1 st.
Knit into front and back of this st to make 5 sts.
Next row: Knit.
Next row: Purl.
Next row: Knit.
Next row: Pass second knitted stitch over the first and then the next and then the next until one remains. Fasten off. Run a gathering thread around the outside and form into a small ball. Make 2.

Stitch to the ends of the arms.

Tail

Make as for the paws but using white 4-ply cotton.

Scarf

Using 2.25 mm double-pointed knitting needles and blue wool, cast on 3 sts. Work in garter st until your scarf is long enough to knot around the rabbit's neck. Make a small fringe and attach to each end using a wool needle or a crochet hook.

To Make Up Stitch the head to the top of the body ensuring the nose is pointing forwards. Sew the ears in place, making a small pleat at the bottom to help them stand up. Centre the tail on the back, a little

higher up than the legs. Attach the arms to the shoulders. Knot the scarf around the neck. Sew the legs to each side of the body so that he sits on the hat. Using black embroidery cotton, stitch the eyes using straight stitches or French knots. Sew a pink nose with pink embroidery cotton.

Flowers

Using 3 mm crochet hook and 4-ply yarn, make 6ch, join with ss into a ring.

Round 1: (right side) 1ch, 11dc in ring, using contrast colour ss into first ch of round (12 sts).

Round 2: Continue with contrast colour. (11ch, ss in next dc) 12 times, ending ss in ss of first round. Fasten off neatly. Make 7 in different shades of blue, yellow and white.

Hat

Using 3.75 mm double-pointed knitting needles and mid blue 8 ply cast on 92 sts (30, 32, 30). Work in st st for 10 rounds. Fasten off mid blue and join in bright blue and white 8 ply. Work k2 bright blue, p2 white rib for 12

rounds.

Round 23: Knit in bright blue.
Round 24: Purl in bright blue.
Round 25: Knit in white.
Round 26: Purl in white.
Popcorn Stitch rounds: Work as follows:

Round 1: (right side) *P3, (k1, yo, k1) into same st, rep from * to end.
Rounds 2 and 3: *P3, k3, rep from * to end.
Round 4: *P3, k3tog, rep from * to end.
Rounds 5 and 6: Purl.
Round 7: *P1, (k1, yo, k1) into same st, p2, rep from * to end.
Round 8: K2, *p3, k3, rep from * to last 4, p3, k1.
Round 9: As round 8.
Round 10: Slip last k1 of third needle on to first needle so there is a group of k3 at the start of the

round. *K3tog, p3, rep from * to end of round.
Rounds 11 and 12: Purl.
Repeat rounds 1–6.
Round 19: Knit in white.
Round 20: Purl in white.
Round 21: Knit in bright blue.
Round 22: Purl in bright blue.
Work 2 rounds st st in white.
Work 2 rounds st st in blue.
Work 2 rounds st st in white.
Round 29: Knit in bright blue.
Round 30: Purl in bright blue.
Round 31: Knit in white.
Round 32: Purl in white.
Work 2 rounds st st in mid blue.

Crown Shaping

Crown is worked in mid blue.
Round 1: *K7, k2tog, rep from * to end.
Round 2 and even rounds: Knit.

Round 3: *K6, k2tog, rep from * to end.

Round 5: *K5, k2tog, rep from * to end.

Keeping pattern of decreases continue in this manner until the round k1, k2tog has been worked. Break off yarn. Thread through rem sts, pull up tight and fasten off.

To Make Up

Attach one flower to the centre of the crown and then stitch the rabbit on top. Stitch the remaining flowers around the top of the crown.

Daisy Mouse

This cute beanie is knitted as a tube and gathered at the top like a paper bag. The vertical stripes are easily created using alternating yarn colours. Peeping out is a dear mouse. If you omit the daisies this would be a lovely hat for a boy. The basic pattern is a quick knit.

Sizes

To fit 12-18 months (2-3 years)

Materials

1 x 50 g ball cream DK (8 ply)
1 x 50 g ball French blue DK (8 ply)
Small amounts 4-ply cotton in navy, pale blue, white and fawn
Polyester fibre filling
Stranded embroidery cotton in pink and black

75 cm x 1 cm-wide blue velvet ribbon
Wool needle
Embroidery needles
4 mm double-pointed knitting needles
3 mm crochet hook
2.25 mm double-pointed knitting needles

Abbreviation

Wyib: with yarn in back

Hat

Using 4 mm double-pointed knitting needles and cream, cast on 92 (98) sts.

Join into a ring being careful not to twist sts.

Work 16 (20) rounds of k2, p2 rib.

Join in French blue and knit 1 round.

Work sl st pattern as follows.

Round 1: K1, *k1, sl1 wyib, repeat from * ending with k1.

Round 2: K1, *sl1 wyib, k1, rep from * ending with k1.

Round 3: Using cream k1, *sl1 wyib, k1, rep from * ending with k1.

Round 4: Using cream k1, *k1, sl1 wyib, rep from * ending with k1.

Rep rounds 1–4 until work measures 15 (17) cm from beg ending with row 4 complete.

Cont in French blue only and work in k1, p1 rib for 2 rounds.

Eyelet round: K1, *yrn, k2tog, rep from * to last st, ending with k1.

Work another 10 (12) rounds of k1, p1 rib. Cast off in rib.

Mouse

Head

Using fawn 4-ply cotton and 2.25 mm double-pointed knitting needles, cast on 9 sts (3, 3, 3). Join into a ring.

Round 1: Knit.

Round 2: K1, m1, k1, m1, k1 on each needle (15 sts).

Round 3: Knit.

Round 4: K1, m1, k3, m1, k1 on each needle (21 sts).

Rounds 5-8: Knit.

Round 9: K1, k2tog, k1, k2tog, k1 on each needle (15 sts).

Rounds 10-11: Knit.

Round 12: Sl1, k1, psso, k1, k2tog (9 sts).

Round 13: Knit.

Leaving sts on needle, stuff head firmly. Run thread through rem sts, pull up tightly and fasten off. Set aside.

Body

Use white 4-ply cotton and 2.25 mm double-pointed knitting needles, cast on 9 sts (3, 3, 3). Join into a ring.

Round 1: Knit.

Round 2: K1, m1, k1, m1, k1 on each needle (15 sts).

Round 3: Knit.

Round 4: K1, m1, k3, m1, k1 on each needle (21 sts).

Round 5: Knit.

Round 6: K1, m1, k5, m1, k1 on each needle (27 sts).

Rounds 7-15: Knit.

Round 16: Sl1, k1, psso, k5, k2tog on each needle (21 sts).

Round 17: Knit.

Round 18: Sl1, k1, psso, k3, k2tog, on each needle (15 sts).

Round 19: Knit.

Round 20: Sl1, k1, psso, k1, k2tog, on each needle (9 sts).

Round 21: Knit.

Leaving sts on needle, stuff body firmly. Run thread through rem sts, pull up tightly and fasten off. Set aside.

Ears (Make 2)

Using 2.25 mm double-pointed knitting needles and working backwards and forwards in rows cast on 2 sts.

Row 1: Purl.

Row 2: K1, m1, k1.

Row 3: Purl.

Row 4: Inc in first and last st. Work 2 rows without shaping.

Row 7: K2tog, k1, k2tog.

Row 8: Purl.

Cast off.

Using 3 strands of pink embroidery cotton and satin stitch, embroider the inner surface of the mouse's ear.

To Attach to Head Pinch lower edges together and pin to head. Stitch firmly to sides of head.

Legs and Arms

The legs and arms are made with knitted I-Cords:

Using 2.25 mm double-pointed knitting needles and fawn 4-ply cotton, cast on 3 sts.

Row 1: Knit.

Do not turn, slide sts to the other end of the needle, pull yarn firmly behind the work and repeat the first row. Continue until your I-Cord is 3.5 cm long for the arm. Sl1, k2tog, psso, fasten off.

Make 2.

Make 2 legs in the same way, each 5 cm long.

Feet and Paws

Using 2.25 mm double-pointed knitting needles and fawn 4-ply cotton, cast on 1 st. Mb. Break off yarn. Thread through st. Pull up tightly and fasten off. To form into a bobble, run a gathering stitch around the outside, draw up and fasten off. Make 4 and attach one to each arm and leg.

Tail

Make a 2-stitch I-Cord 6 cm long following the instructions above. Stitch to mouse.

Making Up the Mouse Sew the head to the body with the pointy nose at the front and the widest part of the body as the base. Using 3 strands of black embroidery cotton, make a French knot on each side of the head for

To Make Up

Thread the velvet ribbon through the eyelet holes. Draw up firmly and make a bow. You will now have a little nest for the mouse to sit in. Make sure Daisy mouse is facing the same way as the bow and stitch firmly into position. Sew five flowers around the top of the ribbing, evenly spaced. Sew one on the front and one on the back of the hat.

the eyes and fasten off invisibly where the head joins the body. Using the pink embroidery cotton, make a French knot for the nose. Sew arms and legs in place. Attach the mouse to the hat.

Flowers

(Make 7 in a combination of blue and white shades)
Using 3 mm crochet hook make 4ch, join with a ss into a ring.
Round 1: (right side) 2ch, 9dc in ring, ss to top of 2ch (10 sts).
Round 2: 5ch, 1tr in each of next 9dc, ss to top of 5ch. Fasten off.

To Make Up Sew in ends and form into a neat circular shape.

Embroidery Stitches

Many of the hats included here are decorated with embroidery stitches as well as knitted ornaments. Before embroidering on the hat, try out each stitch first on a spare piece of fabric to make sure you are happy with the yarn as well as the embroidery.

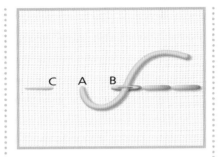

Back stitch

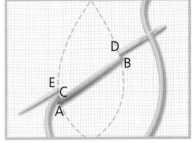

Satin stitch

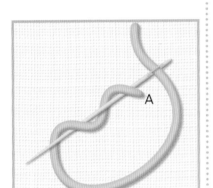

French knot stage 1

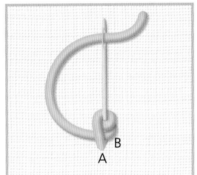

French knot stage 2

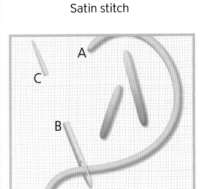

Straight stitch

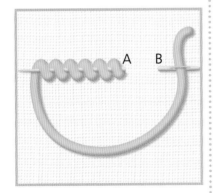

Bullion knot stage 1

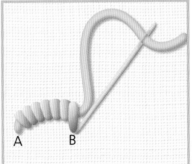

Bullion knot stage 2

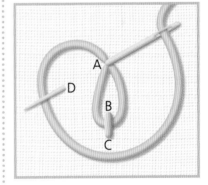

Lazy daisy stitch

Index